D1614332

Culture & Politics in Nicaragua

Photo Credits

José Coronel Urtecho, Pablo Antonio Cuadra, Mayra Jiménez, Ernesto Mejía Sánchez, Beltrán Morales, Alvaro Urtecho by Steven White; Ernesto Cardenal, Alfonso Cortés, Fernando Gordillo, Ricardo Morales Avilés, Joaquín Pasos, Leonel Rugama, Solomón de la Selva, Daisy Zamora courtesy of the Ministry of Culture, Nicaragua; Carlos Martínez Rivas by Claudia Gordilla; Roasrio Murillo by Nancy Pierce; Sergio Ramírez by Carol Wells; Rubén Darío, *The New York Times*.

Cover: Catalina Parra

Steven White

Culture & Politics in Nicaragua

Testimonies of Poets and Writers

Lumen Books

Acknowledgments

Grateful acknowledgment is made to the following editors and publishers for permission to reprint in this book certain portions that originally appeared elsewhere:

Another Chicago Magazine for the interviews with Mayra Jiménez and Daisy Zamora.

Commonweal for portions of an interview with Ernesto Cardenal by Ronald Christ.

New Star Books Ltd. for portions of *Christians in the Nicaraguan Revolution* by Margaret Randall, translated by Mariana Valverde.

Northwest Review for the interview with Pablo Antonio Cuadra.

Third Rail for the interviews with Sergio Ramirez and Rosario Murillo.

For their invaluable direction and guidance, the translator would like to thank the following people: Jorge Eduardo Arellano, Ronald Christ, Suzanne Comer, Juan Armando Epple, and Uri Hertz.

Lumen Books
446 West 20 Street
New York, NY 10011

Printed in the United States of America
ISBN 0-930829-06-9 Hardcover
ISBN 0-930829-02-6 Paperback

Contents

¿Seremos entregados a los bárbaros fieros?
¿Tantos millones de hombres hablaremos inglés?

Crees que la vida es incendio,
que el progreso es erupción;
en donde pones la bala
el porvenir pones.
No.

Rubén Darío

Culture and Politics in Nicaragua: Defining a National Identity

This collection of testimonies from Nicaraguan writers is a mixture of interviews, key documents, and speeches. The material provides a diverse panorama of the evolving intellectual conscience of Nicaragua over the last sixty years. I hope that the book will help educate English-speaking people about Nicaraguan culture and that it will contribute, in a small way, to a different kind of interdependency between the United States and Nicaragua. This new relationship must be based on an understanding of the political, linguistic, and cultural barriers that traditionally have divided the Americas.

In countries such as those in Latin America that are subject to the necessity and the possibility of complete social transformations, the personal life of the artist is becoming increasingly linked with the collective life of his people. Until recently, Nicaragua, for example, was considered a backward, semi-feudal country run by a political strongman. Now Nicaragua is at the forefront of Latin America's political vanguard. Since the Somoza dictatorship was overthrown in 1979, Nicaragua has embarked on a search to establish a new political and cultural identity. Under these conditions, social changes inform not only the personal development of the artist but also the cultural evolution of an entire country. There is a general distrust of politicized art in the United States, perhaps because we have grown accustomed to the smooth substitutions of Democratic for Republican administrations and vice versa. In our educational system, there is often a separation of culture and politics based on the belief that they are, by definition, mutually exclusive and antagonistic. We are taught that the proper subject matter of a poem does not include the political.

Many poets in the United States have challenged these tenets in recent years by discovering that a good poem depends not on a particular theme, whatever it may be, but on the writer's skill. And so, using Whitman, perhaps, as a spiritual guide or a poet from another country whose work has been translated into English, poets in the United States have been exploring and expanding the boundaries of politicized language. Examples that come to mind include the moving contributions by Carolyn Forché, Galway Kinnell, Denise Levertov, and C. K. Williams in Stephen Berg's anthology *Singular Voices*, the verse in *Carrying the Darkness: American Indochina—The Poetry of the Vietnam War* edited by W. D. Ehrhart and the valuable range of essays collected by

Richard Jones in *Poetry and Politics*. The true cultural diversity in the United States is manifesting itself in writing by Native Americans, Blacks, Hispanics, Asians. Political concerns regarding the environment, Gay rights, feminism, U.S. foreign policy and the anti-nuclear movement have become prominent themes in new poetry.

The issues raised as to how Nicaraguan artists produce their art within or on the fringe of the political realm goes beyond the current topical interest in Nicaragua. The material gathered here, though limited in its scope to twentieth-century Nicaragua, contributes to an understanding of a more universal context—individual artists and their relationship to power. Throughout history, there have been poets at the side of the powerful, poets serving the state and its diverse cultural projects, poets falling from grace and banished, poets praising the new power or challenging official culture and its way of ordering reality. From Callimachus to Propertius, from the anonymous authors of the *Book of the Tao* to the poets collected in the Manyōshū, and the political exiles Ovid, Dante, Voltaire, and Pushkin, poets often have been embroiled in the political struggles of their times. In our own century, there are the examples of Mandelstam and García Lorca. Mayakovsky and Marinetti sang the praises of two emerging powers. Breton, Pound, Brecht, Vallejo, Miguel Hernández, Seamus Heaney, Akhmatova, Neruda, De Rokha, Nazim Hikmet, Hans Magnus Enzensberger, Ferlinghetti, Ginsberg, Amiri Baraka, Wole Soyinka, Dennis Brutus, Roque Dalton, Otto René Castillo, and Heberto Padilla are all poets who, in their own ways, helped define the relationship between culture and politics.

Nevertheless, Nicaragua has its own particular context. Consequently, *Culture and Politics in Nicaragua* is a history that documents different social/cultural trends by way of the country's literature. The book is divided into four sections that reflect key periods and individuals: Poets of the Vanguardia; The Generation of 1940; The 1960s and '70s: A New Militancy; and, After the Revolution. The voices of the poets predominate because poetry traditionally has been Nicaragua's richest means of cultural expression. In fact, poetry is so important in Nicaragua that it transcends the realm of the arts to become a fundamental basis of national identity. It was not hyperbole when Ernesto Cardenal, Nicaragua's Minister of Culture, wrote that Rubén Darío was "the greatest *geographical* event in Nicaragua." That is to say, Darío's *modernismo* was a revolution in poetry that put Nicaragua on the map in the nineteenth century and established Hispanic America's literary independence from Spain.

One of the principal forces influencing the cultural development of Nicaragua is the foreign policy of the United States. Since the 1823 Monroe Doctrine, the United States has clearly defined its opposition to outside interference in the Americas as well as its own hegemony in this hemisphere's affairs. In terms of respecting Nicaragua's national sovereignty, not much has changed from the time of William Walker, the adventurer from Tennessee who invaded Nicaragua in 1855, declared himself president, reinstituted slavery, and proclaimed English the official language. Inscribed on the banner of Walker's small army was the slogan ''Five or None''—a reference to the five countries of Central America. The current administration in the United States is playing for the same stakes with a parallel fanaticism.

Nicaraguans have no reason to expect any other form of treatment from the United States. Howard Taft sent the Marines to occupy Nicaragua in 1912; Calvin Coolidge sent them again in 1926; when the troops were withdrawn in 1933, owing mainly to the tenacity of Augusto César Sandino and his poorly-armed, barefoot guerrilla army, the United States installed the Nicaraguan National Guard under the command of Anastasio Somoza García. This initiated nearly half a century of dictatorial rule by a single dynasty supported by eight successive U.S. presidents.

Culture and Politics in Nicaragua begins with two writers, now in their seventies, who began to publish their work in the highly politicized ambience of Nicaragua in the late 1920s and early '30s. This literary generation, which later became known as the *movimiento de la vanguardia*, made a brief but intense incursion into politics. Although the Vanguardia began as a movement that, for nationalistic reasons, backed Sandino's struggle, the Conservative social background of the Vanguardistas led them to distrust democratic solutions. For some of the same reasons that attracted Yeats, Pound, Eliot and Stevens to Mussolini and Fascism in Europe, members of the Vanguardia felt that what Nicaragua needed was a ''healthy'' dictatorship. Therefore, they decided to sign a manifesto supporting the person who was at that time the young head of the army—Anastasio Somoza—in order to take power with him and thereby realize their cultural and political ideals. They assumed that it would be easier to conquer one man than to conquer a people.

At the other end of the ideological spectrum was another Nicaraguan poet, Salomón de la Selva (1893-1958). He directed (in English, in the United States) a fierce campaign in favor of Sandino and against Somoza. He wrote numerous articles that appeared in magazines such as *The Nation*, *Panama America*, and

Latin American Digest.

The purpose of the material gathered in this book is not to satisfy the reader's hunger for the life behind the artist's work, but to expose the complexity of the life/art problem in Nicaragua, where political changes have produced corresponding cultural changes so deep that there is no middle ground in a person's artistic or political life. Furthermore, as Terrence Des Pres points out in an excellent study of Bertolt Brecht: " . . . when art becomes overtly political, we have some right to suppose that how the artist conducts his public life will certify or jeopardize his work's authority; and we may also suppose that excellence, while it excuses much, cannot condone its own betrayal." Ernesto Cardenal, the most well-known member of Nicaragua's Generation of 1940, exemplifies the tension that exists between a poet's life and the literary merit of his work. Because of his commitments as an official spokesman for the Revolution, a role that he is trying to relinquish on account of its demands on his time, Cardenal has written relatively little poetry for the last decade. Critics have taken a hard look at some of his most recent poems published in the beautifully printed book *Tocar el cielo* (To Touch the Sky). These are testimonial pieces with revolutionary and utopian themes that are sometimes weakened by their lack of what Robert Bly, in describing the best political poetry, has called "an especially fragrant language."

As Minister of Culture, Cardenal has defined the overall cultural project in Nicaragua as "the democratization of culture." He explains that before the Revolution an elite group produced their art for a small, well-educated public while the majority of Nicaraguans remained illiterate. The Sandinistas have taken two actions designed to change this situation. First, they have enacted literacy campaigns that have enabled a large percentage of the population to learn how to read. They are also printing books in inexpensive editions so that more people have been able to purchase books published since the Revolution. But, as far as the leadership is concerned, more remains to be done. According to the founder and former director of the popular poetry workshops, Mayra Jiménez, these measures and others allow greater access to culture, but, nevertheless, art still may be "for" the people instead of "from" the people. The goal is to distribute the *means* of cultural production more equitably and thereby change the relationship between the creator and the consumer of culture. In Nicaragua, an elite that had produced art "for" the people can no longer claim this exclusive right. A sector of Nicaragua's population that had been uneducated and ignored now has the chance to express itself through the arts and to receive a modicum of recognition.

An illustration of this priority can be found in the Ministry of Culture's promotion of the popular poetry workshops. Mayra Jiménez points out that "the poets in the workshops all have proletarian origins. They're campesinos and workers. . . . They're all combatants. The experience that forms the major emotional burden at this time is still closely related to what was going on before, during and after the war." In this sense, the workshop poetry has a therapeutic value for the participants and, to the extent that it captures an important part of Nicaragua's immediate past, an historical value as well. Because of the war on Nicaragua's borders and the panic-inducing sonic booms from low-flying U.S. spy planes, many Nicaraguans believe that the role of the artist cannot be confined to the solitary production of art. As Rosario Murillo, head of the Sandinista Association of Cultural Workers, states in her interview: "We have to be ready militarily—just like the rest of the people—to defend this revolution, with weapons in our hands. But we also have to defend it as artists. And so we go to the different fronts of the war in cultural brigades to do theater, poetry, and painting for and with the soldiers. And if we have to go into combat, then we'll do it." The material presented by the cultural brigades also includes folk dancing, humorous plays, and music. In addition to being a welcome gesture of support for the troops, it is also an educational experience for the participating artists. A member of the Germán Pomares Cultural Brigade, sent to the Honduran border, told me of overcoming his fear as he recited a well-known poem by Rubén Darío, "¡Eheu!," to eager soldiers who had grown accustomed to the intense machine-gun fire all around them. The poem and its references to "being and non-being, and fragments of consciousness from now and yesterday" had never before meant so much to him, even though he had learned the poem by heart as a boy. On a hill on the other side of a river, he saw contras quietly lay down their weapons. People from both armies were laughing at the end of the show and the spell was not broken until the contras, before they realized what they were doing, began to applaud. Then all hell broke loose.

This kind of cultural activism was described in another way by Commander Tomás Borge, who said that the triumph of 1979 was the result of a revolution "made with guitars and poems, and with bullets." The statement is true in both a figurative and a literal sense when one recalls the didactic lyrics of songs that circulated during the insurrection and taught the general population how to load rifles and manufacture homemade bombs. In defining an artist's commitment, with its variety of meanings, young Nicaraguan artists must assimilate in their own lives the examples of the rebel poet Rigoberto López Pérez, who gunned down the elder Somoza at a party in León in 1956, and of guerrilla poets such as Leonel Rugama, who was murdered by the National Guard at the age of twenty in 1970.

For Sergio Ramírez, Nicaragua's recently elected Vice President and most well-known novelist, the Revolution was as much a cultural victory as a political one. Nearly fifty years of Somocismo meant the transplanting of an imported cultural model. "The United States," says Ramírez in his interview, "wanted to give us the gift of tons of *Reader's Digest* magazines to make us thoroughly anti-Communist. But, worse than that, they wanted to turn us into mediocre thinkers."

On the other hand, intellectuals who disapprove of the Sandinistas, such as Pablo Antonio Cuadra, poet and editor of the opposition newspaper *La Prensa*, are concerned about a Cuban/Soviet influence and entering into what Cuadra calls "a decadent imitation of what's been realized in those culturally gray countries whose socio-economic results are far from being a successful model." Cuadra, in his interview, also addresses the critical issue of creation versus censorship in a highly politicized society.

The scope and structure of this book are a continuation of the studies that led to the publication of my bilingual anthology *Poets of Nicaragua: 1918-1979* (Unicorn Press). Several trips to Nicaragua over the last six years and a brief visit to Mexico City enabled me to compile the material contained in the present volume. The interviews with Pablo Antonio Cuadra, Ernesto Mejía Sánchez, Beltrán Morales, Daisy Zamora, Mayra Jiménez, Alvaro Urtecho, and Rosario Murillo were tape-recorded in single sessions of varying lengths. I later transcribed the tapes, edited them in Spanish for the sake of coherency, then translated them into English, always attempting to uphold the spirit of the conversation as I recalled it. The interview with Carlos Martínez Rivas was condensed from ten to twelve hours of conversations recorded on several different occasions. When subjects preferred to submit written responses to my questions, as in the case of José Coronel Urtecho and Sergio Ramírez, I asked them to try to maintain an anecdotal rather than an academic quality in their answers. The section on Ernesto Cardenal is composed of excerpts from several major speeches and parts of interviews conducted by Ronald Christ and Margaret Randall. The contributions of Omar Cabezas on Leonel Rugama, Ricardo Morales Avilés, and the round-table discussion are drawn from published sources identified in the introductions to each of these sections.

Culture and Politics in Nicaragua does not seek to highlight personalities or establish the importance of certain voices over others. It is simply a way of demonstrating how generations of Nicaraguan writers consistently have tried to metabolize the experience of history in order to stay alive. In a recent *Paris Review* interview, Carlos Fuentes describes how Pablo Neruda used to say that "every Latin American writer goes around dragging a heavy body, the body of his people, of his past, of his national history." This book attempts to recreate the "heavy body" of Nicaragua's political and cultural reality for the North American reader.

I. Poets of the Vanguardia

José Coronel Urtecho

José Coronel Urtecho, born in 1906, was one of the founders of la Vanguardia, *an iconoclastic literary movement that began in Nicaragua in the late 1920s. In 1927, Coronel returned to Granada, Nicaragua, from San Francisco, California, where he had been exposed to new trends in North American literature. The members of the Vanguardia included Coronel, Luis Alberto Cabrales, Pablo Antonio Cuadra, Joaquín Pasos, and Octavio Rocha. For Nicaragua, this group signified an authentic national renaissance. The Vanguardia sought to create a literary language capable of combating the empty solemnity and flowery verse written by Rubén Darío's untalented imitators. This new poetry used conversational language, collage, free verse, dialogue, satirical humor, and innovative linguistic music from traditional and popular sources. The Vanguardistas were also avid translators. Through a collective effort, they presented the poetry of Rimbaud, Apollinaire, Cendrars, Pound, Eliot, and Williams. In addition, they published poems by many writers of Spain's so-called Generation of 1927.*

The members of the Vanguardia came from Conservative families that had been displaced from power by the Liberal reforms of President José Santos Zelaya, who seized power in 1893 and ruled despotically until 1909. The labels "Conservative" and "Liberal" conform to their definition in Nicaragua (and throughout Latin America) in the nineteenth century. The Conservatives were associated with the feudal, land-holding oligarchy, while the Liberals sought to modernize the country by consolidating the large estates; investing in roads, railways, and shipping; revamping archaic legal and administrative institutions; and creating a national bourgeoisie by means of a strong domestic market. In Nicaragua, this process of liberalization was halted since Zelaya's nationalistic and protectionist policies ran counter to the United States' strategic interests in the region. The United States intervened in 1909 and helped the Conservatives overthrow Zelaya.

The members of the Vanguardia did not reject the bourgeoisie as a social class; but, rather, the "bourgeois spirit," which signified commercialism and anti-intellectualism. The Vanguardistas, through insolence, extravagance, and controversial writing, hoped to abolish the vulgarity and mediocrity of the money worshippers' non-culture.

In addition, the social background of the Vanguardistas made them doubt that a democratic system of government could solve the social, economic, and political problems of Nicaragua. Luís Alberto Cabrales had recently returned from France with materials about the Action Française and works by Charles Maurras, including Enquête sur la monarchie. *The Vanguardistas were undoubtedly familiar with Marinetti's brand of Futurism in Mussolini's Italy. European Fascism confirmed the anti-democratic, elitist ideals of the Nicaraguan Vanguardia, which saw in Somoza a man capable of transcending partisan interests and rebuilding Nicaraguan culture. As Coronel wrote in 1975, in his political memoirs entitled* Mea máxima culpa*: "We thought we could orient Somoza toward the good of the country and the Nicaraguan people without understanding, due to our inexperience, that it was impossible."*

Coronel held various jobs as a functionary of the Somoza government from the 1930s through the 1950s. Gradually, as the disastrous shortcomings of the dictatorship became more evident and subsequent generations of writers aligned themselves with the growing opposition to the Somoza family, the Vanguardistas individually withdrew their support from the dictatorship.

Jorge Eduardo Arellano, Nicaragua's foremost literary critic, has said that José Coronel Urtecho is "our most lucid man of letters. Without his written and oral work, contemporary Nicaraguan literature cannot be explained." Coronel is a classic example of how culture in Nicaragua is transmitted from one generation to the next—not in the context of universities or academic settings, but in direct conversations. Many writers have made the journey to "Las Brisas," the farm where Coronel lives and continues to write.

One of Coronel's books of poems, Pol-la d'ananta katanta paranta, *was organized and published by another Nicaraguan poet, Ernesto Gutiérrez, in 1970. Taken from Homer, the title means "and through many ups and downs, comings and goings," aptly describing the verbal musicality and the constant literary experimentation in Coronel's work. This book contains one of his most difficult poems, "Retrato de la mujer de tu prójimo" ("Portrait of Thy Neighbor's Wife"), which is a kind of Joycean nightmare. His only other published book of poetry is* Paneles de infierno *(Panels of Hell). It is an excellent example of "exteriorist" poetry, the "objective," "revolutionary" verse promulgated by Ernesto Cardenal.*

For this interview, José Coronel chose not to submit himself to the rigors of a tape recorder and preferred to write his responses to a limited selection of questions that I had prepared. Although the answers address the symbiotic relationship between culture and politics in Nicaragua, they are somewhat unsatisfying in that they fail to capture the marvelous transcendence of the poet's spoken words. On the occasions I visited the poet at his farm or at the Ministry of Culture in Managua, he was carrying a wooden cane and wore the long-sleeved white shirt, dark pants, and beret that are his trademark.

What has been the effect of the foreign policy of the United States on the cultural development of Nicaragua?

One can't speak simply about a "foreign policy" of the United States in relation to Nicaragua. It's an anti-Nicaraguan or counter-Nicaraguan policy of the United States in Nicaragua, made by proconsuls who are sometimes Nicaraguans—like the Somozas. These people were the real ambassadors of the United States in Nicaragua who directed even the North American ambassadors themselves. The United States' "foreign policy" in Nicaragua is abominable, interventionist, colonialist, and imperialist. It has violated our sovereignty and has been destructive to all that's Nicaraguan.

You lived for a number of years in the United States and wrote a book about your experiences entitled Rápido tránsito *(Rapid Transit). How would you characterize the people of the United States?*

I'd say there are various "North American peoples" or sectors of North American people, who differ, not only from one group to another but within each group as well. They are linked only by an external and superficial system and are sometimes even opposed to each other. For many reasons, I only believe or have confidence in the poets and artists of the United States (whom I admire a great deal) and not in what is called the "people" or, in other words, the population of the United States. A famous German professor at Columbia University was once asked in my presence if he believed the United States was a great people. He answered: "The United States may be great, but it isn't a people."

Several decades ago, you and Ernesto Cardenal published your Antología de la poesía norteamericana *(Anthology of North American Poetry). You also wrote an extensive essay entitled "Panorama de la poesía norteamericana: 1745-1945" (Panorama of*

North American Poetry: 1745-1945). What initially attracted you to the poets of the United States?

Perhaps what attracted me at first to North American poets was that their poetry, for me, was not just poetry but poetry relevant to the personal and popular life in an American country. When I say "America," I mean the American continent.

What did you learn from Pound?

I learned from Pound what all the poets of our time learned from him: to be poets authentically, and to be poets in our moment and situation and language. As far as I can tell, Pound appeared at a critical moment, not just for the English language but perhaps for all Occidental languages—maybe even the non-Occidental ones as well. I've discovered that he had quite a bit of influence in Japan. But this stuff about influences is always relative and should be blended into each particular case.

Does this have anything to do with the subtitle of your book Pol-la d'ananta katanta paranta*: "imitations and translations"?*

The majority of the poems in that book are "imitations and translations." I don't think the translator is always a traitor as the Italian saying goes, but, sometimes, a co-author in another language, in another medium, another situation.

What is the origin of the distinct language in "Portrait of Thy Neighbor's Wife," a poem written in the 1940s? Certain critics have spoken of a "spiritual crisis."

I believe that the different "language" of that poem has to do with the fact that what it expresses could not be expressed, cannot be said, perhaps, in another idiom except that "language." I used to say that it was in "tongues," due to the style of the poetic text. The "Portrait" is, of course, an oneiric poem made, really, during a dream in a dreamed language—but written while awake. My later attempts to imitate it were nearly all trance-like, but not dreams. I don't know how to simulate dreams.

You've written a great deal about the history of Nicaragua. You founded and helped direct the newspaper La Reaccíon *in 1934 that was openly anti-democratic, in favor of Somoza and a totalitarian system of government. In February of 1980, you wrote the long poem* Paneles de infierno, *an unrelenting indictment of Somoza and U.S. intervention in Nicaragua that you dedicated to the Sandinista Front. Given this evolution in your political thought, how has your own historical experience changed your perception of Nicaraguan history?*

I did not continue writing about history because I lost faith in history. I lost faith in the past and in history as the past. I realized, in addition, that I did not know, nor could I learn, our history, much less write about it. All our Nicaraguan history, the written one and the one we lived, is false and cannot *not* be false. The only true history of Nicaragua is the Sandinista, anti-imperialist Revolution: truly Nicaraguan. The other history is, at best, the history of Spain and the history of the United States—except, of course, the almost unknown history of the Nicaraguan people, which is the pre-history of the Revolution. The only history that can be ours is what makes our Revolution. All the rest is false in itself—and falsified. That was the truth that I learned in my failed attempt to write about history. Because of the Revolution, now we can write history as we make it—and that's the true history. This history identifies itself with truth and poetry. The three things are *one* in the Revolution: history, truth, poetry. By making poetry, now we are making history.

Do you believe in miracles?

Everything is a miracle, as Walt Whitman says in his short poem "Miracles." I believe only in miracles; in what's not a miracle, there's no reason *to believe*. A poem, for example, is a miracle. A poem, in addition, is a miracle that converts everything it touches into a miracle.

Where does the concept of exteriorist poetry originate?

Exteriorism has its origin in the poetry of Ernesto Cardenal. Its extra-Nicaraguan antecedents can be found, for example, in Pound, the Imagists, and William Carlos Williams.

Could you say a little about Carlos Martínez Rivas and compare his poetry to Ernesto Cardenal's?

To say "a little" about Carlos Martínez Rivas would take me at least a book and I can't write books anymore—nor have I ever been able to write a book. I didn't even put together my book of poems *Pol-la d'ananta katanta paranta*. Ernesto Gutiérrez did. The other books signed by me aren't really mine and some of them I repudiate today. Even *Rápido tránsito* is almost entirely "imitations and translations." When I say about Ernesto Cardenal and Carlos Martínez Rivas that one is a tiger and the other a bird of paradise, I suppose I mean that they can't be compared.

What projects are you working on now?

I'm working, as always, at trying to work—and preparing myself to die properly.

Pablo Antonio Cuadra

Pablo Antonio Cuadra's poetry is fundamentally Nicaraguan. This is as true today as in 1934 when he published his first book, Poemas nicaragüenses *(Nicaraguan Poems). His stand at that time against the invasion of U.S. Marines, in an early poem such as "Poem of the Foreign Moment in the Jungle," is much the same as in "The Calabash Tree," from his most recent book,* Siete árboles contra el atardecer *(Seven Trees against the Dying of the Light).*

Cuadra was born in 1912 and traveled as a young man with his father throughout South America. In the 1930s he was actively involved in the cultural and political projects of the Vanguardia, and his opposition to Somoza García led to his imprisonment in 1937. He was imprisoned again in 1956 when the elder Somoza was assassinated. At that time, Cuadra was co-editor, with Pedro Joaquín Chamorro, of the newspaper La Prensa. *His political opposition to the Somoza regime intensified during the 1970s, years that deeply affected the poet: the National Guard assassinated Pedro Joaquín Chamorro in 1978, and* La Prensa *was destroyed in 1979 by Somoza's troops during the final offensive. Since 1980 Cuadra (now editor of* La Prensa*) has come under increasing attack from the Sandinistas as a "counter-revolutionary," owing to his upholding of a "democratic bourgeois" tradition.*

This interview was conducted at the poet's home in Managua in July, 1982. The statue of Jonah in the belly of the whale, located by the front door, took on a special political significance, considering Cuadra's conflictive relationship with the powers that be in Nicaragua. During the three-hour conversation, Cuadra alternately smoked a pipe and cigarettes. He spoke calmly, surrounded by countless shelves of books, and meditated on his words. His occasional gentle laughter seemed to distance him from subjects about which he held strong opinions. Afterward, as I was about to leave, Cuadra gave me a bag of mangoes that he had picked from a tree in his backyard. I was reminded of Cuadra's poem "The Mango Tree," which refers to a Chorotega Indian belief that the brightly-colored mango is the soul of the chichiltote*—a sacred bird that caught fire as it flew to the sun.*

What was Granada, Nicaragua, like in the 1930s? Were you born there?

Actually, I wasn't. When I was about to be born, my father was employed in Managua in the government, so I was born in Managua, on Candelaria Street, where my father had a house. When I was four, we returned to Granada. He was from Granada and my entire family has lived there for centuries. I always lived there, too, until my work at *La Prensa* forced me to stay in Managua. For a long time, I worked at *La Prensa* and commuted every day by car from Granada. I didn't like leaving Granada. It's very beautiful.

It has changed quite a bit, hasn't it?

In a certain way, it has, because it has gotten better. A lot better. They started building little houses in good taste, with a certain style. On the outskirts of the city, the houses are much prettier now than when I was young. The same is true of the streets. The streets used to be made of sand. That's one of the things that made Granada different. People used horses and carriages when I was young, and it was the custom to go for a horseback ride in the afternoon. Later, after the arrival of the automobile, people stopped using horses. In almost all the houses of a certain social rank, there were stables right next to the house and a servant who took care of the horses. We used to go for rides along the shore of the Great Lake of Nicaragua. You're reminding me of some things I had almost forgotten—that life when I was a child.

What effect did the Lake have on your poetry?

I think the Lake is one of the primary muses in my poetry. Let me tell you something. I lived through the December 1972 earthquake here in this house in Managua. It was incredibly traumatic to see the whole city destroyed. And it was a real blow to experience the stealing and dirty things organized by Somoza and the National Guard, as well as the commerce with pain and death.

At that time, I had a little piece of land in Granada, on the shore of the Lake. I had built a house there and I think that returning to the Lake was a kind of cure for me. The majority of us who suffered through the earthquake suffered the same emotional experience. But for some it came gradually and in different ways. I remember how some friends made fun of me when they saw me hanging my head and being sad. But about five or six months later, they fell into the same melancholy state. Take Rosario Murillo, for example. Six months after the earthquake, I found her crying over her typewriter, and I asked her: "What's the matter?" She had lost a little boy. He was killed when part of the house fell on him. But the emotional effect on her didn't occur until months later. There wasn't anyone who, in some way, didn't feel the blow. It's difficult to understand without having lived through it: what it meant when all of a sudden an entire city just ended, along with all of a person's established friendships. And I realized how much a neighborhood and friends influence one's sense of emotional order. Life seems woven together by what surrounds us. Knowing that a person lives in a certain place and that other people get together in a certain café is our way of joining the vital threads. When all this suddenly ends, it's a kind of death. Even though you don't die, something inside and outside you dies.

But I was talking about the Lake, wasn't I? I was telling you how just staying there and listening to the maternal song of its waves took the trauma out of my life. It freed me from the captivity of my mind. My eyes and heart belong to port towns. It always depresses me a little when I arrive in a city that has no horizon, that's enclosed. I'm used to the broad horizon of a port city. I like to feel like a neighbor of the Lake.

When did you start to write?

I really began when I was a boy. When I was in the fourth grade, I had a teacher, a young Jesuit named Miguel Pro, who probably noticed that I was imaginative and decided to make me write. He told me to write for him instead of attending class. I wrote what I did with my friends on vacation and I drew for him. He liked what I did and made me do more. I wonder what those first manuscripts were like? That's what awoke in me the vocation of expressing myself through writing. I remember that priest saying: "Today, Pablo Cuadra will stay after school." He took me and some other boys to some nearby farms or to the woods where we hunted, picked fruit, and walked along the roads. The next day he told me: "You aren't going to do the grammar composition. Write me a story about what you did." And he forced me to do it. That's what happens sometimes: the first exposure.

Were there other writers in your family?

Perhaps not that many writers, but many intellectuals. My father was an orator and a writer as well. He wrote about history, not literature. Among my ancestors was a poet, a priest named Desiderio Cuadra, who wrote a lot of poems in the style of the eighteenth century. Another relative was the poet Manolo Cuadra.

Manolo's whole family has written: José Cuadra Vega, Luciano. My family has produced many intellectuals, some writers, and not one general—thank God.

In the 1920s and '30s, at the beginning of the Vanguardia movement, which writers had the most influence on your poetry?

From Nicaragua, very few, with the exception of Rubén Darío. My father knew Rubén, read his work and talked about him a great deal, because when Rubén came here to Nicaragua to die, my father was the government person in charge of taking care of him and giving him money owed him by the previous government. Rubén Darío touched all Nicaraguan writers in one way or another.

You once said that Alfonso Cortés was a disciple of Quirón, the centaur in Rubén Darío's "Coloquio de los centauros" (Colloquium of the Centaurs). Is that because there are certain metaphysical traits in Darío's poem?

All the questions, the anguish, and the metaphysical concerns of Quirón are contained in that dialogue between the centaurs. Alfonso continues them, converts them into his vital and poetic philosophy. But it's not just that, although this is the root of Alfonso's metaphysical leap. It's extremely interesting how a suggestion of anxiety concerning certain themes in a poem like "Colloquium of the Centaurs" could create an entire mentality in another poet who was the "son" of Rubén Darío—a son he drove crazy.

Were there other Nicaraguan modernista *writers who influenced your early work?*

I did know some of the *modernistas* and read their work, but I wasn't very impressed. I'm talking about when I was a boy. Before I got the idea that I was going to be a writer, I read solely for pleasure—mostly adventure stories. Afterwards, it was different. Ramón Saenz Morales visited my father's house. And because I knew him, I read his things in newspapers and magazines. And Lino Argüello, a relative on my mother's side, was a truly romantic character, a pallid, timid, weak man who signed his name "Lino de Luna." He was an aristocrat, a drunk, very delicate, with the hands of a prince. His clothes were dirty, torn, and his shirtcuffs were ragged, but when I went to León, he recited his poems to me because he knew I liked that. Later, I read and became close friends with Azarías Pallais. But that was when I began writing in the time of the Vanguardia. And who else? If there were any others, they were bad writers who never attracted me but were well known in Nicaragua. When I began to study literature at school, I read a lot of Amado Nervo as well as other romantic and modernist poetry. That was the age when I went around being in love. I read Nervo, the inevitable Bécquer, Lugones, Herrera Reissig, and (because of the Jesuits) Virgil, whom I read in Latin. But the time comes when a person finds himself and wants to distinguish his own personality. That's when I reacted against Darío and all the previous reading I had done. And then we all began to look for "the new." What was new had an immense value in our generation. The generation of the Vanguardia was born with a cult of "the new." Sometimes it was exaggerated.

In what sense?

In that we excessively rejected anything that wasn't new. We wanted to create something new at any cost. I can only compare the extremism of my youth with the next generation of poets in Nicaragua. I watched Carlos Martínez Rivas and Ernesto Cardenal grow up, and they didn't have the uneasiness and restlessness that marked us. All of us who were working together to form the Vanguardia movement—José Coronel, Joaquín Pasos, Octavio Rocha—shared this same belief. The poets of the next generation entered into their time without hostility, receiving and following the current. We didn't. There was a rupture and a search for what was new. At that time, French poetry influenced me a great deal, because, first of all, French was a language I more or less had mastered. Second of all, Apollinaire and company opened doors to the unkown for me. I never learned English, unfortunately. I began to look for books and became familiar with the new French writers. My friendship with José Coronel and Luis Alberto Cabrales, who had just returned from France, helped me a great deal. We began to read these new writers and to translate them. In me, the French influence was more marked; in Coronel and Pasos it was the English. I became slightly familiar with English through the reading I did with them. We had an advantage over other writers in that we had formed a group of friends—a team. Whoever didn't know a language got help from someone else since we met to read and translate together. That's how I became quite familiar with North American poetry—more than I realized at the time. Later, poetry from other languages was opened to us through these two languages. That was something really good about the Vanguardia: we gathered the masters who were going to guide us in the invention of our own literature. And without a doubt (even though we didn't realize it at first) we owed this instinct to seek the universal to Rubén Darío. We were never a group of provincial poets writing about church steeples. We wanted to see what was going on in the world, assimilate it, and then create our own poetry. And we did that instinctively, even when we were young. There were a lot of movements parallel to ours and I was familiar with many of them. Because I traveled as a young man, we had contacts in Chile, Uruguay, and other Latin American countries. I found that some groups were closed off and had fallen into a kind of provincialism. Their language was an isolated, poor vernacular. This was true in Uruguay, where I found a nativism that was too regionalistic. That seemed asphyxiating to us. Deep down, we were followers of Rubén. We wanted to join the cosmopolitan with the national.

So, the Vanguardia wasn't really against Darío but against his falsifiers?

Yes, that's true. At the beginning, we attacked him a little, but that was very short-lived. We attacked the part of Rubén we considered evanescent and dangerous—things that were too precious and exotic. We wanted something more direct. We believed that this ornate poetry with its language like gold filigree had been surpassed and that we could discover a new kind. Later, we realized it was Rubén himself who was pushing us forward. That's the truth. His kind of genius has such an infinite variety of traditions that it wasn't until later that one discovered them. The modernists discovered one Darío. Lorca and Vallejo discovered others and later declared themselves children of Rubén—and they *were*, even though they had their anti-Darío side as well.

The members of the Vanguardia were never very far from political territory, were they?

At the beginning we were. Later—and this is something I'll always blame on José Coronel, for better or worse—it was different. He got us into a political venture that now seems absurd to me. I was never very sympathetic to the reactionary utopia that Coronel spoke to us about with a fantastic array of verbal and ideological pyrotechnics. Coronel, as my literary godfather, was exceptional. But as my political godfather and political adviser . . .

well, he never hit the mark, never. For this reason, his influence was ominous in the same way that his cultural magistry was stupendous. And this is how it happened. We were discovering our own literary sources by investigating popular forms and folklore. We wanted to extract what was Nicaraguan from the language of the people so we could know and affirm our cultural identity. So, Coronel began to study history. Since we virtually lived and breathed literary meetings and gatherings, Coronel told us: "Let's study history. It'll be good for you. Read this book and underline such and such a thing for me." So we got involved with history in a belligerent and argumentative way—against this, that, and the other. That's where he got the idea of involving us with politics.

Of course, we were living in a highly politicized atmosphere, and we reacted against it. And in our cult of the new, we wanted to get involved in a new kind of politics that was against what had gone before. Fascism had a greater influence over some of us. In others, such as Coronel, the doctrine of Ramiro de Maeztu and of Charles Maurras and the Action Françcaise was more influential. We were obsessed with a nationalism that we wanted to be ultra-original. And, of course, Communism repelled us, because our movement was nationalistic. We were a movement parallel to Sandino, and the Communists at that time were deeply internationalistic. In Nicaragua, during their first public demonstrations, the Communists burned the Nicaraguan flag and sang the "Internationale." And that repelled us. We were disgusted with Stalin's Russia from the start. This feeling pushed us into sympathizing with anti-Communist movements even though socialism and Christian communalism attracted us.

I don't know what kinds of conclusions we would have reached, but when I look back on those years when I was with Coronel and involved in that political venture, I can see what a loss it was for my poetry. I'll never forgive myself for that. But those were also fruitful years because the sins and errors of youth are the best experimental base for a mature and balanced intelligence. It was difficult, given the high level of politicization in Nicaragua, for us not to get involved in politics. Rubén, while he lived in Central America, also swam in the currents of his time and suffered more than a few confrontations as a result. But in our case, what was bad wasn't the fact that we got involved in politics in order to invent something new. Nor was it bad that we wanted to formulate an ideology based on a number of influences (some very bad) and original concepts (some very good). The problem was that at a certain moment José Coronel Urtecho convinced us to sign a manifesto supporting the person who was at that time the young head of the army—Anastasio Somoza—in order to take power with him and realize our political ideas. Coronel's machiavellian thesis was that it would be easier to conquer one man than to conquer a people. Somoza said that he would make our ideas his. What he really did was deform them and take advantage of our idealism. He showed his claws soon enough. A few months later, I was imprisoned after being accused of putting up posters in honor of Sandino. It was a joy for me because I learned my lesson. And from that time on, I was against Somoza. Coronel, on the other hand, believed that as far as political tactics were concerned, personal feelings should play no part. That's why he subscribed to Somocismo all his life. This venture, as I told you, cost me a long period of poetic sterility. From *Poemas nicaragüenses*, which I revised a great deal in 1935, to *Canto temporal* (Temporal Song), I produced hardly any literature. I do have one little book, *Cuaderno del sur* (Southern Notebook), which I wrote but didn't publish, containing about ten poems from the trip I took to South America. It later occurred to me that they were greatly influenced by French poetry about traveling at that time. I read the book later and I've decided—if I don't change my mind again—to include it in a possible anthology of my work. *(Revista del pensamiento centroamericano* [No. 177, Oct.-Nov. 1982, 9-24.])

These poems are from the mid '30s?

Between 1934 and '36, more or less. Just a few poems I had always put aside, perhaps out of respect for Joaquín Pasos, our great traveling poet who never traveled.

You were close to Joaquín Pasos. What was this most precocious member of the Vanguardia like and what caused his early death, at the age of 32 in 1942?

Joaquín was, I believe, the greatest poet we've had since Rubén Darío. He had a freshness and an extraordinary creative ability. Perhaps the person most like him in regard to that ability and gift is Carlos Martínez Rivas. But Joaquín had more freshness and joy. He was an extrovert and very happy. Carlos is a little wrapped up in himself. Joaquín wasn't. Nor did he have the kind of self-image that would have made him annoying. He was always really friendly. The two of us, along with Octavio Rocha, made the Vanguardia movement, along with other people who eventually contributed to it, after Coronel left.

When Joaquín was a boy, he was sick with typhoid and that injured his heart a little. It seems as if that sickness stayed with him—secretly. And Joaquín really liked to party as a young man. He was a sparkling, imaginative bohemian. He drank a lot, stayed up all night, and went everywhere. God knows, a party with Joaquín Pasos was something serious. It was impossible to keep up with him. And little by little, he wasted away. When I went to Mexico in 1945, we had just finished editing his book *Breve suma* (Brief Summation). I wrote the prologue and helped him pick the poems. The book was at the publishers, Nuevos Horizontes, half-finished when I left. At that time, when we were working on the final selections, he didn't look well to me. His ankles were inflamed and he was very tired. He went to see a doctor in Costa Rica. Joaquín asked him: "Doctor, can I have a drink once in a while?" "Yes," he replied, not knowing first of all that Joaquín was a wild-man and secondly that he never drank "once in a while." So, Joaquín was cut loose, and that's why he died. I was in Mexico at that time, so they sent me the prologue to finish, since the last pages had been lost. That's how *Breve suma* came to be published.

In what sense is Joaquín Pasos' poem "Canto de guerra de las cosas" ("Warsong of the Things") a "Christian defense of man's dignity"?

I think in the sense that it assumes man's pain, exalts the nobility of that pain and raises what is human against war and everything that destroys us. He does this by putting the feeling of compassion and solidarity into language. This poem was born in Nicaragua after Eliot's *The Waste Land* and rectified its desolation with a disconcerting humanism. But the rest of America hasn't recognized the value of Joaquín's poem. It's one of the great poems of our time. If Joaquín Pasos had been Mexican or Argentine, he would be in all the anthologies. Today, Joaquín occupies a certain place in the history of literature. But it has always been thanks to our efforts of insisting on his value, never forgetting him, sending his work to anthologies and rescuing him from oblivion. To us, he is "Adonis"—the eternal youth. Carlos Martínez Rivas wrote "Canto fúnebre a la muerte de Joaquín Pasos" (Funeral Song for the Death of Joaquín Pasos), and he used it as a calling card in Spain. Luis Rosales and Leopoldo Panero were very impressed when Carlos read it to them. Ernesto Cardenal has also worked on and for the poetry of Joaquín Pasos. He wrote the prologue for the edition of Joaquín's work published by the Fondo de Cultura in

Mexico.

Reflecting on your own poetry, what have you done with "the mud of history"—the image you use in your poem "Poema del momento extranjero en la selva" ("Poem of the Foreign Moment in the Jungle")?

I think I've contributed, whenever possible, to the poetic values of that other, secret history of our people—the one discoverable in myths, folklore, language, and customs. The poet gathers and embodies the marginal life in language. He gives it new meaning, he "consecrates" it, defends it with irony and hope. I'm not a messenger; I'm an interpreter. I fight to take on the eyes of the people, to "see" with them what the people see: their realities and their visions. My prophecy is simply hope. I don't lead; I'm in communion with my people.

During the period when you wrote Temporal Song *you said, "I had faith in the Faith, but this decisive encounter with Christ revealed to me the faith in Love." My question is, how is this encounter with Christ different from Ernesto Cardenal's?*

Cardenal's encounter was more generous than mine. He surrendered himself and gave up everything (including his poetry) to enter a Trappist monastery. This is something serious. What could be called "the Cardenal problem" came much later. When he went to Cuba, he became very enthusiastic about Communism and entered an accelerated process of Marxism that carried him, in my opinion, to a dangerous politicization of his religious faith. I call it "dangerous" because politicizing religion immediately produces fanaticism. Nevertheless, I'm not the one who can make comparisons and evaluations about the two encounters. Let's leave that judgment to Christ.

But I can give you my opinion of Ernesto's human side. What has made me suffer about him is his dehumanization. The gentle man of the monastery has been replaced by the hard dogmatism of an ayatollah: once again, the cross with the sword. I committed that sin as a youth. I don't want to make the same mistake as an old man. I will say this: Cardenal is holding on to a high voltage wire—something you've got to be very careful with. I'm talking about prophecy. He considered himself a prophet and, at first, did it well; but later, he *believed* he was a prophet and fell into the kind of self-security that has prompted him to raise himself above others and judge them. Ernesto is no longer my friend. He is my judge. A short time ago, while talking in Germany with a writer who was concerned about Ernesto's evolution as a writer, I said that these days there are two great writers who have been carried away emotionally by prophecy: Solzhenitsyn and Cardenal. The Nicaraguan is obsessed with Communism ("Communism is the kingdom of heaven," he wrote in one poem). He sees Communism as the solution to everything, the millenary kingdom of justice on earth, Paradise within our reach. Solzhenitsyn leaves the experience of Communism to announce the Apocalypse to the world. The Russian is returning from the same utopia where Cardenal is heading and "sees" the opposite: Russia and the West are crazy and suicidal powers, bent on destroying each other through enslaving technology, depersonalization, monster-states, torture, murder, pollution, and the destruction of Nature as well as the last freedoms of humanity. Cardenal is Hope with closed eyes; Solzhenitsyn is Disillusion with open eyes. But the interesting thing is that both are products of the same phenomenon. "Paradise" and "Hell" are in the same place.

Could you tell me a little about the poetry from Temporal Song*? To what do you attribute such a distinct use of language?*

Temporal Song demanded a change of poetic language because it is a poem of introspection, of autobiographical confession. But it's also about the arrival on the beach of poetry after a shipwreck. In that sense, even though with a greater mastery of expression, the poem "El Hijo del hombre" (The Son of Man) is a continuation of the same spiritual state and of the same language that, without a doubt, differs from my prior work and also differs from what follows.

Because, more or less at the same time, José Coronel was writing poems such as "Retrato de la mujer de tu prójimo"—a poem that has certain surrealist traits.

At that time, possibly, we were both reading a series of books and talking about things that created some special atmosphere and provoked the different treatments of surrealism in our respective poems. I don't recall precisely what we were reading, but I do remember that Coronel was in Granada. I went there in the afternoons and read him parts of the poem as I wrote it. Coronel commented on it. I needed that kind of dialogue because it was a long poem of great breadth. will say, nevertheless, that *Temporal Song* had a torrential "inspiration"; the clouds gathered after a period of drought and I wrote it without resting. Since then, I've never been solicited by that need to review my life and confess it as a kind of liberation.

A spiritual crisis?

Yes. With the melancholy of youth, with a melancholy that still is dynamic and optimistic, the poem reflects my lost dreams and defeats. But among the remains of the shipwreck, the poet discovers that he has salvaged what's most important: Love. After I finished the whole thing, I also read all of *Temporal Song* to Joaquín Pasos. I went to Managua for that sole reason. It made a deep impression on him—above all, the final Christian part. Perhaps Joaquín was also in a critical moment and sensed his own approaching death. He made me read him the last part more than once: the songs of the "man-Christ" who comes to life after his defeats, the part where I say that "the cross is a broken door." Joaquín quoted that metaphor to me in one of his last letters.

Jumping to another theme, do certain problems arise when you try to combine your two professions—journalist and poet?

I've said it many times: the influence of journalism on my work doesn't exist, except in a narrative way. The only thing it has done is put me on the defensive as a poet. I never wanted to be a journalist and perhaps I let myself become trapped because I had certain skills as an editor. I've always liked the art of typography, and I was always starting up and directing some kind of publication. Ever since I was little, even when I was in high school, I put out small poetry magazines by hand. But I knew that was very different from a journalist. I recognized the well-defined border, even in the concept of time—a border that a writer fears. Don Pedro Joaquín, the father of Pedro Joaquín Chamorro, offered me the possibility of working with him several times. I was also offered a job as editor of another newspaper called *La Estrella de Nicaragua*. But I preferred a life of relative poverty as a farmer or "shepherd" as I said then. Later, in 1952, I got involved in a venture—planting cotton—that went poorly for me. That decided my fate. Don Pedro Joaquín eventually called again and asked me to be co-editor of *La Prensa* with his son. And I accepted.

Luckily, I was prepared for the job. When I was living in Mexico, from 1946 to 1949, Pedro Joaquín, Jr., was studying law there. As a personal favor, he asked me to help him undertake a practical study of journalism: "I want to study the newspapers in

Mexico in relation to those in Nicaragua. I want to compare them and see what new things I can introduce into *La Prensa* when I start working there after my return." So, we invented our own journalism course. We collected Mexican newspapers, studied them, analyzed their text, graphics, headlines, sections, etc. and then, comparing them with what we had in Nicaragua, we wrote down the things we could introduce back home. I never thought this was going to be useful to me. At the time, I was working as a columnist for the newspaper *Novedades* and other periodicals to earn my living while I put together a publishing house. Then I brought Pedro Joaquín Chamorro, Jr., to the newspaper where I worked and we learned the physical and administrative aspects of running a big newspaper.

In 1954, when I started to work at *La Prensa*, which was founded by Pedro, the first months were terrible, because the work devoured all my time and left me none for my own writing, which was all that mattered. I began to develop a kind of conscious and subconscious defense about finishing what I had to do as a journalist so I could go home and work on my books. It was very difficult. Ever since then, I've always been on the defensive about being a journalist. Always. That doesn't mean I've always been victorious. Often my work tires me out so much that I come home and don't feel like writing or, sometimes, even reading. Besides, it's not very good to write a few things here and a few things there. On weekends, though, I refused to work on the paper. Pedro instituted the Sunday edition, and I told him: "Don't count on me. I have to take care of my other work." I never worked on Sundays. "Never on Sunday," as the song says. One has to give the imagination a large space so it can wander and roam.

Do the poet and the journalist have different responsibilities in balancing truth with imagination?

I was never a reporter. I only wrote editorials. When I began at the newspaper, I was an editor. I'm sure that if I had started out as a reporter, the conflicts would have been different. But thinking in the terms of an editorial, analyzing facts and ideas, and saying what you think about a situation don't clash with the imaginative functions of a poet. And little by little, I developed an editorial column that was a mixture of philosophical thought and poetry: humanistic, motivating, historical. It wasn't really a political editorial every day, although I did have to write those when Pedro was put in jail and I had to take over his responsibilities. But as soon as Pedro was released, I gladly gave him back the everyday editorial work.

In 1964, at Pedro's suggestion, I started a kind of editorial column called "Escrito a Máquina" (From the Typewriter). I wrote every Saturday, for years, on cultural themes, political philosophy, historical commentary, etc. This weekly work was useful because it made me study my problematic times in depth. I read a great deal and what I read later showed up in my poetry. I also studied our history and our indigenous cultures to the extent that I put together perhaps one of the best libraries in Nicaragua on ethnography, archeology, and other subjects related to American Indian cultures. From those studies emerged the book *El jaguar y la luna* (*The Jaguar and the Moon*). I learned a lot. That was when I founded the Central American University, where, for several years, classes were taught on the history of indigenous culture for half the course and on ancient cultures of the world for the other half. I also studied mythology, anthropology, and linguistics. I owe everything that has enriched my poetry to those studies. I'm passionately involved in the recovery and incorporation of the Indian into our poetry.

But, yes, there is a contradiction between being a journalist and a poet. To all the writers who came to me wanting to be journalists I said: "If you can be anything else, you'd be better off." All the poets I brought to *La Prensa* failed me in the sense of being good reporters. Perhaps they were never able to invent an informative genre connected with poetry: a lack of imagination on their part or of understanding on the part of the editorial staff. I don't know. More than a contradiction, there's a kind of hostility between journalistic and poetic time.

In 1956 you were imprisoned for having worked on the opposition newspaper at the time of the elder Somoza's death. And without a doubt La Prensa *had great influence as an opposition force during the dictatorship of Somoza Debayle. What has been its role since 1979?*

We collaborated with the Revolution. We participated in it. We produced all the propaganda possible in the most subtle but constant way to favor the revolutionary movement's getting rid of Somoza. That means we were allies of the *Frente Sandinista*. We knew all the commanders of the Revolution. With some of them, such as Tomás Borge, I maintained clandestine relations. This was our revolution, made possible by everyone. We did our part right up to the end: anguish, life under threat of death, the destruction of the paper and the death of Pedro Joaquín Chamorro.

After the triumph of the Revolution, all the pluralist forces decided upon a constitutional compromise, the Fundamental Statute, which set down the basis for the creation of the new economic, social, and political life that the Revolution would bring to Nicaragua. Our work at *La Prensa* has been to defend this statute against the deviations from it that occurred later. But I must tell you that right from the beginning the commanders of the *Frente Sandinista* were not open to criticism: they didn't want us to criticize them at all. In other words, freedom hinders them. It *hinders* them. Yet, when we defeated Somoza, didn't we defeat dictatorial government and replace it with a government open to dialogue? A closed mentality contradicts the root and essence of the revolution the commanders brought about themselves.

Another cause for the clash between *La Prensa* and the commanders is our desire to commit ourselves to promoting a process of democratization, of self-determination. Ideally, a socialist system should function democratically. We're completely open to a process that is not demagogic, but systematic and gradual: we never opposed the process of socialization and agrarian reform. What we do oppose is a state that grows on us like a monster. We never want giants again, whether they are called Stalin, Mao, or Fidel. The history of the twentieth century is too telling for us to allow to go on erecting these absolute powers that end up crushing all of man's liberties. And to impede the monstrous growth of the state or of power, we know of only one antidote: democracy.

We've fought for humanity, for the human dimension. We fought for it, not only because it's the only form of government and socio-political organization that gives one powers against Power, but also because it's the only system by which a revolution—that is, a process of change—can structure an equal relationship between government and people. This relationship must be one of real, free, vigilant, critical participation on the part of the people concerning the decisions that will affect their destiny. Only within a democracy that elects its authorities, who respect pluralism and freedom of expression, can a government function without deception and understand its people's needs.

We want our revolution to be an original one, derived from our Nicaraguan history and that of Hispanic America. That's why we have split from the FSLN—and also because of its foreign policy. In our work, Pedro Joaquín Chamorro and I have exalted the thought and attitudes of Sandino in defense of our sovereignty, against foreign involvement, and against imperialism. When it was formed, the governing junta committed itself with all the revolutionary forces to "an independent and non-aligned foreign policy." That was the national decision: non-alignment! But the Cuban influence soon split that position into factions. *La Prensa* began to be harassed because it condemned this application of Sandino's anti-imperialist thought. The paper supported Panama in its demands on the United States concerning the canal, *and* it supported Afghanistan and Poland against the intervention of the Soviet Union. The junta harassed us, and censored us as well, because we signaled the danger of surrendering ourselves to the game of condoning one imperialism in order to defend ourselves from the other. The independence of a small country, I warned in *La Prensa*, consists in not letting itself become a pawn for other world powers. That has been my position at *La Prensa*. Is it debatable in certain aspects? Fine! Let's make discussion possible. If I am fighting for anything, it's for a non-dogmatic revolution that's open to dialogue.

Has the role of the Ministry of Culture been positive?

In certain respects, yes; in others, no. It has been positive because it has increased the cultural possibilities of the people. It has impelled the democratization of culture with brilliant results; but, at the same time, there has been an overpowering imposition or cultural *dirigismo*—where the state directs everything—demanding that arts and letters place themselves at the service of the Revolution. Which revolution? Only the one defined by the commanders. And there's the problem. They conduct these popular poetry workshops, for example. Just recently there was a program on television about them, and there you could see and hear for yourself—I'm not imagining things!—a young poet saying: "I didn't know until now that my poems were no good because they have no message." Now, in the language of the leaders who indoctrinate the participants in the workshops, just what does that mean? It means that the poems had not been *politicized*. If this criterion is being proposed as an *ars poetica* to a lot of young people, what kinds of aberrations will be produced? Perhaps the boy's poetic sensibility inclines him to write a great metaphysical poetry, like that of Alfonso Cortés. And if you ask a metaphysical poet to write with a political message, you will ruin him. He'll think that whatever comes from deep within him, authentically, is false or mistaken. If he falls into the trap, the lesser poet will try to express what is revolutionary—something he doesn't feel—in a style that is not his. He will rely on formulas or on imitations of others. Another poet may be a great love poet, some Neruda at the early stage of *Veinte poemas de amor* (*Twenty Love Poems*). That kind of *dirigismo* is very dangerous. Besides, after the Russian and Cuban experiences, it turns out to be childish and anachronistic. Wouldn't it be ridiculous for the Nicaraguan people, who have created such a great, original, and American literature, to fall into an inferiority complex that would lead them to imitate what's Russian and Cuban, just because their cultural leaders told them to?

For me, the harm is tremendous that can be done to a people with that "devotion"—inculcated from above—to Soviet-influenced cultures. If not, let me ask you this: has there been a great cultural renaissance in those countries? Where are the great Russian writers? I'd ask the same thing about Cuba. Cuba's great poets are the ones from before the Revolution. Where's the great new work? A lot of young poets have streamed into exile from Cuba. In New Jersey, they even have their own magazine, *Linden Lane*. And it's a good one. Is that what we're going to force when we could have made something marvelous? Are we going to repeat the example of Heberto Padilla and Reinaldo Arenas? This bothers me, and it hurts me deeply that so many young poets come to *La Prensa* and say: "I'd like to bring you my things, but they've forbidden us to publish in *La Prensa Literaria*." Or, "I'd like you to publish me, but I'm scared I'll lose my job." This kind of atmosphere is fatal. It's the Inquisition, the negative culture of prohibition.

About three months after the triumph, there was a round table of intellectuals here. Julio Cortázar came, and there were representatives from each generation—myself, Mario Cajina-Vega, Lizandro Chávez Alfaro, Luis Rocha, and Xavier Argüello—with Ernesto Cardenal presiding. That discussion was wonderful. Everyone, even Ernesto, felt obligated to accept the fact that the cultural base of our revolution was creative freedom. I was very happy. I know that for a person who isn't a creator, who isn't a poet or artist, this fundamental problem is not important. The scribe writes what he's told to write or he uses a formula, and that's that. But the person who carries the sacred fire inside like a torment knows the harm it does. The only reader, the only critic, valid for the poet is his own creative "I". All interference—more so if it's political—and all criticism foreign to the demands of his own work are castrating.

Shall we change the topic?

Yes.

Many Latin American writers, in their search for the universal, create characters who are a kind of collage, a single character from many people. Do you use this same technique in your poetry? I'm referring specifically to characters such as Juana Fonseca and Cifar.

Juana Fonseca is based on a real person to whom I added a little by way of anecdotes and certain imaginative touches that don't correspond to her. The same with Cifar, but I barely knew him. The person who reminded me the most of Cifar was Juan de Dios Mora, whom I knew as a boy and also mention in the *Cantos de Cifar* (*Songs of Cifar*). I heard stories I used for Cifar from other sailors I knew on the Lake. In substance, the essential character is my invention. He's also real. But I think that way of creating characters is universal. The writer, unless he decides not to be, is faithful to a real person as much as he can, given that he is someone else. But, yes, the writer can't avoid putting in something of himself, his own soul or his imagination, which surrounds the character and transforms him into someone else. Take that reflective type, for example, the Master of Tarca. He was based on a carpenter we used to employ on our farm. He fixed boats and built new ones. He was a man who constructed a great deal of philosophy around his sayings—a creator of maxims and language. He was no Sancho Panza, though. He was an elemental thinker with a reflective mind. But to the real man, I added a poetic function. I shaped him into word and linguistic form—a kind of teller of myths.

It seems that Cifar is more a literary/mythological figure than a literary/historical figure, such as a dictator in a novel by García Márquez or Carpentier.

That's precisely what I was trying to create—a mythic anti- or pre-hero who represented the man of the Lake. Everywhere the sailor is the type of the bold adventurer, has many women, constantly confronts danger, etc. That's what a navigator's life creates, no doubt about it. And in the *Songs of Cifar* I write a lot about the sense of being uprooted that one has on the water—the call of "the blue." But through him or with him I try to create a more humble, marginal element, a primitive or naif epic with the characteristics of the sailor I knew when I was young. Remember "The Black Ship" from your anthology *Poets of Nicaragua*?

THE BLACK SHIP

Cifar, in his dream, heard the cries
and the howling conch in the fog
at dawn. He watched the ship
  immobile—
  fixed between waves.

  —If you hear
  in the dark
  midnight
  —in high waters—
  cries that ask
  for the port:
            Turn the rudder
                  and flee

The dark hull, gnawed away,
outlined in the surf,
(—Sailor!, they cried—)
the broken rigging
rocking and the sails
black and rotten
                  (—Sailor!—)

Standing up, Cifar embraced the mast

  If the moon
  illuminates their faces
  ashen and bearded
  If they ask you
  —Sailor, where are we bound?
  If they implore you:
  —Sailor, show us the way
  to the port!
  turn the rudder
  and flee!

They set sail a long time ago
They navigated in the dream centuries ago
  They are your own questions
  lost in time.

I don't know if times have changed much, maybe a little, owing to the way people navigate now. Navigating in sailboats was much more poetic because it gave greater creativity to the sailor. Machinery always depersonalizes things somewhat, and a motorboat just isn't the same. Traveling on the San Juan River in a rowboat, for example, is very different. In one of those motorboats, you're drunk with speed. But in a rowboat, you see a flower here and a bird there, the shoreline, and reflections as you go along. It gives you a totally different experience of nature.

In the process of writing *Songs of Cifar*, I worked hard to balance symbols and realities. I tore up many poems. The same thing happened with the form. I spent a lot of time on it because I wanted to write the poems in short lines, with a certain rhythmic reminiscence of popular forms, but without stifling my own sense of meter. I wanted to find some measure of the epic, but without the solemnity.

How do you explain the combination of Greco-Roman and indigenous mythology in your most recent book?

From the time I wrote *Libro de horas* (Book of Hours) in 1964, I've been preoccupied with something that has pursued me throughout my poetry: the incorporation of the indigenous tradition as well as the Greco-Roman tradition that comes to us through the Spanish language. (Of course, at first I knew a lot less about what I was doing. One learns how to create that fusion, that mestizo-like combination, little by little.) These two traditions seem extremely rich to me and I see no reason why we should cut them off. What we should do is absorb them, give them unity because we, as mestizos, are their synthesis. The Greco-Roman tradition is more accessible through our language: by speaking Spanish we keep speaking Greek and Latin. The indigenous is more difficult because it has scarcely been expressed in language and what there is becomes a challenge. But this challenge, I believe, inspires creativity and opens mysterious zones of human thought and feeling that the western world, with its excess of rationalism, has forgotten. All these myths, scarcely expressed in indigenous sculptures and ceramics, all those embryonic poems that one discovers in a glyph, in a primitive painting, or on a clay pot are like mysterious words that still haven't been formulated.

I remember writing an article about Tikal entitled "The Mute Athens," because Tikal has all the force of Athens but is *mutis*, silent. Therefore, the poet can speak through his imagination, increasing his "I," although it helps a great deal to have had an apprenticeship with the highly creative myths of Greece. America is Athens *and* Tikal: a mythic dialogue for the future man.

This challenge of the mestizo has always fascinated me. What's more, the mestizo continues creating language. Underlying our Spanish are certain syntaxes and indigenous linguistic structures that, through a symbiotic relationship, renew the Spanish language. There's also a large quantity of indigenous words that are myths in and of themselves: word-myths, like some Greek words. The Nahuatl language, especially, is very rich. It contains many words like bullets—they explode with an enormous charge of poetic reaction.

Can you give me some examples?

Here's one from Nahuatl that's fairly well known: *Quetzalcoatl*, which unites two words—exactly like some Greek words—reality and dream, bird and serpent. In other words, it unites an entire philosophy, an entire mythic structure: the highest humanistic achievement in America encapsulated in one word. It's as if Quijote and Sancho could be fused into a single, dual symbol: reality and *sur-réalité*. Another example of a word-poem is *Malacatoya*, which is the name of a Nicaraguan river. Etymologically, it is related to the cranking device used to lift a bucket from a well. I think *Malacatoya* is the perfect name for a river that twists and turns, just like a *malacate*.

Now, there is a phenomenon in the cultural process of Hispanic America—especially in countries with a strong indigenous tradition—that is worth observing, but I don't think has been much studied. The farther literature goes from its Indian-mestizo origins, the closer it moves *toward* these origins for its originality. In other words, we discover the Indian in a direct relation to our distance from him. It's a contradictory but very interesting process in our literature. At the beginning, we hardly even saw the Indian. The eye didn't perceive him. The Indian was mute in our interior exile. The mestizo was ashamed of him. Now—and this is the work of Rubén Darío—the Indian has come into his own. We had to pass through a stage of going beyond the great prejudice against *mestizaje*. It was thought that *mestizaje* degraded a culture and a race. In opposition to this, Rubén became father and teacher. He proclaimed the glory of being mestizo. Through him we recovered our wholeness with pride. And from that moment on, Hispanic American literature was enriched immensely. Enormously. The revolution that came after Rubén was a creative awakening in all genres. Each person discovered his own Indian and his own Spaniard and formed a new being filled with both antiquity and future. This "new world" awareness also appears in the way we speak. We stopped being "pure" linguistically in order to become creative and adventurous.

You once told me that your magazine El pez y la serpiente *(The Fish and the Serpent) is immortal. When will the next issue come out?*

The next issue is at the printer's. I call it "immortal" because it represents and is the fruit of a development of our literature that has hardly ended. It's our "other" revolution: that of the word. Besides, in Nicaragua, where the circulation of books is slow, it's one way of enabling people to become familiar with our national production through a serious, well-selected magazine. That's why I haven't let the magazine become politicized or lose its tradition of independence. If someone writes a political poem, fine; but the magazine's only criterion is quality. Free poetry. Free humankind. Free dreams.

That's the name of the poetry magazine published by the Ministry of Culture: Poesía Libre *(Free Poetry).*

And do you know where they got the title? We used to have a section in *La Prensa Literaria* called "Poesía Libre." I hope that title overcomes the prevailing obsessions and fanaticisms.

My last question, Pablo Antonio, is: can you describe the face of Nicaragua right now?

It's difficult, because it's still taking shape. Right now I'd say the face looks most like Janus—a double face. A double face of forces, some wanting to take us toward one tendency and others wanting to take us toward another. It seems as though a struggle between an ideology and a culture has been produced. I'm almost sure—even though I may not live to verify it—that the originality of what's Nicaraguan will prevail. I hope my optimism isn't groundless. It would be unforgivable if a people capable of creating, if not a complete culture, at least cultural elements that are increasingly powerful and personal, were obliged by force to live in an imported, totalitarian system: a system that imposes everything from thought to uniforms, from what the people should shout to the message a poem ought to contain. We produced Sandino, the great guerrilla, for example. Sandino was a creator.

There must be something behind his worldwide appeal. We have produced not only a Rubén Darío but also a poetic tradition that is original and vital. I don't think this vein has been exhausted, so why should we fall into decadent imitation of what's been realized in other, culturally gray countries whose socio-economic results are far from being a successful model?

But, for the moment, we are still in the eye of the hurricane. Any kind of prediction is difficult. Think about the Mexican Revolution and how it has changed from the beginning to today. Think about what Cuba will be like when Fidel Castro disappears. (Considering what happened with Mao in China, the questions about post-Castro Cuba are immense.) A revolution isn't what's said over the microphones by nine commanders. It's an entire people's long process of change guided by history, individuality, and a deep awareness of human dignity and freedom. My commitment to our Revolution has always been to the people of Nicaragua, to their continued freedom, their basic rights and their hopes. I'm not on the side of power, formulas, or "big words." I'm on the side of humankind. I think that's my obligation as a poet and a Christian.

II. The Generation of 1940

Ernesto Mejía Sánchez

Born in Masaya in 1923, Ernesto Mejía Sánchez, along with Carlos Martínez Rivas and Ernesto Cardenal, is a principal poet of the so-called Generation of 1940. The most recent of the more than 100 books he has published, Recolección a mediodía *(Recollection at Noon), collects poetry written between the 1940s and 1980. Two sections of this book, "Vela de la espada" (Vigil of the Sword) from the 1950s and "Poemas dialectales" (Dialectal Poems) from 1977-1980, show the poet's changing conception of the language of politicized poetry. A rigorously ethical tone of voice underlies his movement from a symbolic to a more overt way of speaking. The synthesis of the dialectical process of his poetry is precisely the Nicaraguan "dialect" in the more recent poems, which contain lyrics to a folk song, a catalogue of cities and villages in Nicaragua, and the voice of Sandino talking about his temporary female companion during the U.S. Marines' siege of Sandino's mountain headquarters in 1927-1928.*

I interviewed Mejía Sánchez in Mexico City in August 1982, at a time when the Mexican economy had just collapsed. The interview was, for the most part, a guided tour through the museum of Mejía Sánchez's house: signed first editions of Neruda, paintings by Balbuena, Mérida, and Gascón, as well as the poet's collection of antique sardine cans.

Do you consider yourself a political poet?

Well, here in my new book, *Recolección a mediodía*, I have whole sections of political poems. What we had wanted all our lives was to get rid of that dictatorship, so the country could enter an age of progress—intellectual progress as well. Morally, even though we didn't take up arms, we used the weapons of poetry. As Tomás Borge said: "The Revolution was made with guitars and poems, and with bullets." That's what we've been involved in. And even though I'm outside the country, here in Mexico, I've always been at Nicaragua's service. For example, I went to Madrid to a congress of writers in July and was elected as a representative of the Latin American constituency because of a document I presented in favor of human rights and the people of El Salvador. On the other hand, I can't leave Mexico on the spur of the moment because of all the things I have here—you'll see my huge library, which is a disaster now, and my collection of paintings. I don't want to expose myself to an invasion, and I'm not going to take everything I've accumulated over thirty years just so it can be destroyed.

I know that you wrote a poem from Recolección a mediodía, *"The Tiger's Spots," in the '50s. But isn't it a universal poem that also applies to the current situation in Central America?*

That poem really is a political poem, written during Franco's regime; but, yes, the spots are poets—all poets:

No one can ignore
the message we form
that makes our anger visible.

We decorate the useless destroyer,
the descent of kindness with no motive.
We burden the delirious
resentment. We are carried without being consulted.
We are nothing more than spots. Pure
spots carried and brought by
the non-government of the bloodthirsty.
Beauty bearing the blame
of its creature in rebellion.

How does this type of political poetry differ from Cardenal's?

This particular poem of mine is more symbolic. The section of *Recolección a mediodía* called "Vigil of the Sword" contains other poems like it with implicit rather than explicit language. I wrote them in the '50s. But afterwards I wrote political poetry that was more insulting and made use of a leaner language. But even these poems, in the "Poemas dialectales" section, are not what Cardenal seems to have taken for a formula. "Exteriorism": only what can be seen should be sung. And for Cardenal it works wonderfully. But I can't deprive myself of the other, intimate part. I conjugate the things of objective life with my spiritual life.

Have you and other poets suffered any consequences because of your political stance against Somoza?

In "To the Poets in Exile" I mentioned the name of Sandino for

the first time. That was in 1954, when Ernesto Cardena
volved in the April Rebellion—a failed attempt to assass
elder Somoza. The dictator later condemned me becaus
poem I speak about a "certain projectile." Someone told
that I was the intellectual author of the plot. After Somoza was assassinated two years later, I wasn't allowed to enter Nicaragua—from '56 to '66. When the people who were involved in the April Rebellion were in prison, Carlos Martínez Rivas was asked by Somoza's newspaper, *Novedades*, to organize an official cultural event. And he did it. I describe this in my poem "To a Poet of the Regime":

Now that you use your Cervantes,
your French, your Péguy, everything
you've learned, heard, and written
in praise of the tyranny,
let us celebrate your crime.

Do you think Carlos Martínez is a relic of another era—the Renaissance?

He is a man of great self-taught culture. He has only read the things that tickle his fancy. Like Baudelaire. But he's not interested in having the big picture of culture. He's like a hummingbird that lives on the best flowers and the best honey in the world. With a lot of genius and sensibility, he's been a freelancer of literature. But I think his cultural panorama is very motley and absolutely unconnected. In his poems, he passes from one literary reminiscence to another. He thinks the reader is obligated to know the map of those interests and those cultures that Carlos has absorbed completely. The perfect example of that is the poem "Two Murals: U.S.A." And there's something else about Carlos that people have accepted just because it comes from him. Since he hasn't had the linguistic and philosophic preparation that Cardenal and I have, he doesn't realize certain things about Spanish as it is currently used. He writes a language that is practically archaic, that comes from books. Cardenal and I, on the other hand, try to write with an absolutely normal syntax.

What about the predecessors of the Generation of 1940? What factors contributed to the political formation of the Vanguardia?

Because of the anti-imperialist/Sandinista atmosphere in which the Vanguardistas lived, they were hunting other things. They didn't find what some other parallel generations in Latin America discovered: socialism, Marxism, the APRA party in Peru, etc. They were seeking what was traditionally Hispanic in order to oppose imperialism. They were looking for folklore, *romances*, riddles, and popular theater. Through that Hispanicism and nationalism, Pablo Antonio Cuadra and José Coronel Urtecho contaminated themselves with Franco's political beliefs. At the time, there was a kind of universal ambience of fascism, Nazism, and the Vanguardistas thought they were going to manipulate old Somoza into being a leader of that kind. But the most fascist of them all was Luis Alberto Cabrales. He studied in France and was a friend and reader of Charles Maurras and the Action Française. He was the true fascist. The others were lyrical fascists.

With the current problems concerning La Prensa, *Pablo Antonio Cuadra has been pushed aside, hasn't he?*

No, not pushed aside. He's there in *La Prensa*, working. *El Nuevo Diario* was formed so that Pablo Antonio could join it with Xavier Chamorro and Luis Rocha. I went to several dinners with them when *El Nuevo Diario* was being planned in order to get Pablo Antonio to leave *La Prensa*. It was clear that *La Prensa* was going to pass over to the opposition. But Pablo Antonio started with a very sentimental defense of how he was taking care of the image of Pedro Joaquín Chamorro. What he's really taking care of is the capital of the Chamorro family. Nevertheless, there is another Chamorro, Fernando, who is working at *Barricada*, the newspaper of the Frente Sandinista. The Chamorro family is very divided.

But in Nicaragua isn't Pablo Antonio Cuadra still respected?

Yes, he is well respected.

I've been told that you are a great collector.

It's true. I have my collection of paintings and a great library. I'm also a specialist in spicy sardines. I have sardine cans from all over the world. In Nicaragua and in Central America in general, the sardines people eat have to be spicy. Since in Spain and Portugal sardines are packed only in oil and tomato juice, the French in Marseilles invented a kind of sardine that was spicy. And they sent it to Latin America. It was a great business. They put "Indio Azteco" on the cans, which was a mistake. It should say "Azteca.'' These cans are very rare now. Later they changed the name to ''Indio Moctezuma.'' I also have these indigenous pieces: they're little heads from Teotihuácan. Some of them, like this little frog, are very strange. Once I went with a professor of mine to the pyramids. Afterwards, while we were looking at these pieces, he asked me: ''What were these little heads used for?'' I told him: ''They were aspirins to get rid of headaches.''

Carlos Martínez Rivas

Carlos Martínez Rivas, born in 1924, is recognized as a "poet's poet."

Owing mostly to his reluctance to publish his work in the form of a book, Martínez remains relatively unknown outside Nicaragua and a small group of international writers that includes Octavio Paz and Vicente Aleixandre. The two editions of his only book, La insurrección solitaria *(The Solitary Insurrection), were out of print for many years until Editorial Nueva Nicaragua reissued this important work in 1983.*

*Carlos Martínez is Baudelaire's legacy to the twentieth century. He is the dandy/*flâneur *observing life on the streets of major urban centers, a wandering phenomenologist who is the sum total of everything he sees. Martínez is a modern extension of the Romantic artist, out of place in a utilitarian, technological, and increasingly illiterate society, who perpetuates the myth of the superior creator. In an interview later in this book, Beltrán Morales speaks of how Nicaraguans "tend to exaggerate the genius of Carlos Martínez because in certain ways we would all like to be him." Regardless of the extent to which Carlos Martínez fulfills the role of the* poète maudit, *one feels compelled to allow the "genius" of the poet's art to redeem the recklessness and self-indulgence of his bohemian existence.*

Martínez's poetry is considered by many to be overly hermetic and erudite, with all its literary, mythological, and biblical allusions and its references to certain painters and musicians. Yet the vitality and fictive genius of the poetic language used by Martínez are derived to a large degree from common everyday events: a woman entering the automatically-opening glass doors of a department store or a little girl watering the lawn. The finished poem is a metamorphosis of those occurrences. It is a good example of poetry as defined by George Steiner in After Babel*: "A poem concentrates, it deploys with least regard to routine or conventional transparency, those energies of covertness and invention which are the crux of human speech."*

In Nicaragua, Martínez is a legendary character whose extreme and stubborn expressions of his individuality have been tolerated and supported by governments of opposing ideologies. Martínez's resolutely apolitical stance, while it may have been acceptable to or even compatible with the Somoza government, is certainly an anomaly in Nicaragua since 1979. Nevertheless, in recognition of the poet's great contribution to Nicaraguan literature, the Ministry of Culture awarded him the Rubén Darío Po-

etry Prize in 1984.

To the best of my knowledge, Carlos Martínez Rivas has never previously consented to an interview. The poet's categorical refusal to submit himself to a tape recorder and a series of questions was difficult to overcome. The first attempt was disastrous: Carlos single-handedly polished off almost an entire bottle of rum in less than an hour. A later attempt also failed when the poet suddenly announced that he had an important meeting—a party at a neighbor's house—and left. The success of the third try, then, came as a complete surprise. Our conversation lasted nearly seven hours as a result of a fortuitous set of circumstances that included a lack of transportation and a violent storm. The interview also contains material from two later sessions. It begins with the poet describing his ongoing bout with alcoholism.

I've gotten a little better. I've been taking Ativan. But my supply ran out and my body had gotten used to its dose. I have my inner workings as well. As it turned out, I found myself helpless last night. When the vodka and rum withdrew from my body, quite early, the anguish of being alone in bed began. I started to toss and turn, toss and turn, and I felt worse than I had in years. I thought I was going to die.

And you didn't call anyone?

No. Let a person die alone, don't you agree? If there's one insomniac, why should there be two? One has to bear that alone. When I had my heart attack in Madrid in 1969, the thing that worried me the most was how difficult it would be to move a coffin up and down the stairway. That's the only thing I thought about. What a practical person I am! They would have had to take me out in a sheet. I started to look at the dimensions of the stairway. Those architects didn't take death into account. I didn't know that I had had the heart attack until years later when the doctor gave me a general examination and found a very severe scar on my heart—dead flesh. And he asked me: "What's that from?" "Ah!" I said. I had written in my diary everything I had felt. And it was the heart attack. At that time my concern was the complication it would cause the owners of the house—the nuisance of a cadaver. But later I wrote down everything I had felt until I called the woman with whom I had some hospital insurance. I finished my narration at that moment. I remember that it seemed as though I were in the United States, because as soon as I hung up the telephone—a few minutes later—the doctor appeared. "Ah, no," he told me. "You probably suffer a great deal on account of your children, you're lonely, and what's more, you've dedicated yourself to writing. We all know that writers are people who are rather abnormal in terms of emotions. You suffered a scare, but it's nothing more." In my diary on that date I described how I approached a mirror and my eyes no longer saw—which meant that I was already dead. I was very pallid and couldn't see. I left the door open and went to bed, ready to die. Something similar happened to me at the school called the INTECNA (Instituto Tecnológico Nacional), where I live in Granada, that I don't want to happen to me now. One day I had an allergic reaction to some vitamins I was taking. Then, I felt much, much worse than in Madrid. I almost lost consciousness. I put on my bathrobe because a friend of mine, Eunice Odio, lay dead for fifteen days in her bathtub. I said: "I don't want that to happen. If I die today at dawn I don't want them to find me like Julius Caesar." According to Thornton Wilder in *The Ides of March*, Caesar covered himself out of modesty when they attacked him with knives. I have a habit of sleeping naked on account of the heat. So I put on my blue bathrobe, left the door half-open and went to bed. But we should get started with the questions.

Okay. One of the things that impressed me the most about La insurrección solitaria *is its coherence, its unity. I'd like to know if you could describe the structure of the book.*

Magnificent question. And I always said the same thing to Octavio Paz. For three months in 1950 and 1951 I accumulated *La insurrección solitaria* in my body. The last poem I had written before that was "Eunice" to Eunice Odio in 1945. Eunice is a beautiful name. *Eunike* means "beautiful victory" in Greek. *Nike* is "victory" and *Eu*, as in the Eumenides, is the prefix for good or kind. The Greeks did not distinguish between the beautiful and the good. Whatever pleases when seen is beautiful. At the same time, it meant whatever is suitable for the self is good. The beautiful and the good were brother and sister. What was good was necessarily beautiful and vice versa. There was no dichotomy like the one that exists now after Christianity established that there were beautiful things that came from the devil. So, returning to the question, I wrote *La insurrección solitaria* in three months. Perhaps in less time. I say three months to set a margin that isn't so surprising. But I think that it was probably in a month. Of course, I had started it when I was in Madrid. From the time I wrote the poem for Eunice in 1945, I remained silent in Spain until Joaquín Pasos died in February of 1947, and then I wrote the poem called "Canto fúnebre a la muerte de Joaquín Pasos." I didn't write anything else except when my friend León Pallais was ordained a priest and I wrote "Romanzón." Those are the only three things I wrote from years and years of experience in Spain. I kept all the exterior and interior stimuli to write inside me. I accumulated poetry and rigor inside me. In other words, emotion and vigilance. I was in Paris. Octavio Paz, Julio Cortázar, and I spent a lot of time together. At that time, we each wrote a book: Octavio, *Eagle or Sun?*; Julio, *Bestiary*; and I, *La insurrección solitaria*. The three works are from 1951, even though I didn't publish my book until 1953, for the same reasons I haven't published *Allegro irato* for twenty-five years. And if it hadn't been for the insistence of Rafael Hueso, *La insurrección solitaria* would still be unpublished.

Was there a lot of exchanging of ideas between you and Paz?

We saw each other. We were friends. One night Octavio invited me to dinner and told me: "I want to give you some original manuscripts, and after fifteen days come have dinner with me so you can return these poems with your comments. Because even though my friends are the best poets in Europe, they're French. Others are Peruvians or Argentines, like Cortázar. You know that the only opinion I trust is yours." I returned the manuscripts to him filled with comments in the margins. That was curious, because when someone asks you for a sincere opinion they don't mean it. The book contained surrealist poems in prose. I called it the immolation of Octavio Paz's talent to his surrealist friends or to the surrealist movement. I thought the book was, in general, poor. So was Cortázar's *Bestiary*. They were European books.

Did Octavio Paz introduce you to the surrealist poets?

All the great surrealist poets were alive and were intimate friends of his. Octavio was already a fairly well-known poet and had his diplomatic position as secretary of the Mexican embassy. He was well connected. Thanks to him, I got to know the great galleries and many poets, among them the surrealist group. I was with Max Ernst, Paul Laforgue, André Breton, Paul Eluard. We went to Breton's house and sometimes his daughter Aube was there, simply ironing in the background. At that time, I thought Breton seemed very old. But it wasn't true. He was born in 1896. In the same year, the great Italian poet Eugenio Montale was also born. *Los raros* was published that year. The year Verlaine died. The same year that Chekov's play *The Seagull* was put on with disastrous results. The coincidences of culture! So, imagine how young André Breton was in 1950. Fifty-four years old. He was four years younger than I am now. I had that contact with him. Once he asked me, "Que faites-vous?" "I'm writing a book." "Oh!" he said with a gleam in his eye and a certain expression of his. He had a striking physiognomy. "I'm very happy to hear that." And it was precisely *La insurrección solitaria*.

What about the structure of La insurrección solitaria*?*

Right. I remember how astonished my friends were when I read them parts of the book every day as I worked on it. It's incredible to think about how I wrote a poem as rich as "The Wise Virgins." After eating dinner at Octavio's place, I started to walk home. I've always been a nocturnal wanderer of great cities. I remember that it took two or three hours. I was walking from the Bois de Bologne on the other side of Paris where Octavio lived in a very elegant house on the Rue Victor Hugo. I was going toward Rue Cassette. He lived on the Right Bank and I lived on the Left. As I was walking, I thought about the poem and when I got to my room it was really late. It was no longer night, it was almost dawn. But I told myself, "This poem isn't going to escape from me. If I don't write it now, if I go to sleep . . . " So, with the enormous fatigue after the night with Octavio, with the fatigue of the long walk, I wrote the poem in one fell swoop. This is how it ends:

The Wise Virgins whispering in the starry bedroom.
Lowering their voices and raising the flame.
Closing themselves in the middle of their shadow.
Disappearing behind their lamp.
Here you have only abyss. Here there is only one fixed point:
the quiet wick burning and the cold halo.
Here you will rip the veil.
Here you will invent the center.
Here you will touch the body
as a blind man touches the dream.

Here you may blow and put out your secret.

Here you may stay and die.

I put it away, very content, and went to sleep. I had left a note on the door, telling the family not to disturb me. The sun was already up when I finished. They woke me at five in the afternoon. I grabbed the manuscript, went to look for two friends of mine, and read them the marvelous poem, "The Wise Virgins."

I remember when I read Octavio Paz another poem I like a great deal—"Saint Christopher." It begins: "*Is there some way across?* shouted the child/ looking toward the dark/ in the ultimate limits/ of brutishness." Octavio said: "Just a minute. Beginning a poem with such expression makes the natural world into something not of this world. It's like the Styx, or Hell." Every day it was astonishing when I read what I had done on the *Insurrección*. The poem "Pentecost Sunday in a Foreign Country" was written in Octavio Paz's house. Octavio was there with his wife Elena Garro, and Ernesto Cardenal, who had just arrived with Ernesto Gutiérrez. Teresita Ramírez, Cardenal's companion in Paris, was also there. The idea was proposed that we each write a poem. It was Pentecost Sunday. We spread out at a considerable distance in Octavio's great mansion. Ernesto Cardenal didn't write anything and Octavio came out saying: "I didn't come up with anything."

What about that part of the poem that says: "And the voluntarily walled city of the self with diamond brow"?

That's Castiglione, Leonardo. The Renaissance man, when there was still individuality.

So the rest of La insurrección solitaria *is from Paris?*

Afterwards, some poems were added in Nicaragua—luckily, since I didn't publish the book immediately, but kept it in a drawer. That was from August of 1951 to August of 1953, when I went to Mexico. Here in Nicaragua, for example, I wrote the epigrams from the world around me—a critique—and put them in the section of the book entitled "The Monster and Its Draftsman." It's the same thing that happens in *Allegro irato*. The book, as a whole, is called *Allegro irato* but has its sections just like *La insurrección solitaria*: "Phantom and Pretexts," "Street Corner with Hope," "Street Corner without Hope," and others. That unity—I'm in complete agreement—isn't a collection that was made after accumulating enough poems, like Darío's *Prosas profanas* or *Cantos de vida y esperanza*. After publishing a series of poems in different magazines, suddenly Darío says: "I'm going to make a volume.'' In my book, everything was done in a solitary accumulation, and then it all spilled out like some kind of bloodletting, as if I had opened a vein. That's how *La insurrección solitaria* was born. In Nicaragua I also added a poem I value a great deal: ''On the Highway the Strumpet Detains the Passerby.''

Where did that title come from?

One day I was in a car with Ernesto Cardenal and other friends. A prostitute named Marina hailed the car. She asked: ''Is Carlos Martínez in there?'' We had a pretty well-known route in old Managua—the Versailles, an amusing place. And listen to this: when my mother died, the notice appeared in the papers: ''Doña Berta Novoa Rivas . . . '' and when Marina took me to her own room where we used to go, I saw she had that picture of my mother on a kind of little altar surrounded by candles with great admiration. Marina. Sometimes I ask myself what happened to those people. They're like myths: nonexistent and at the same time persistent. Nonexistent because they transcend their own person, and persistent because now there's some other Marina, an equivalent. There's always a Persephone, a Demeter, a Venus.

Why does La insurrección solitaria *begin with that mysterious quotation from* El Quijote*?*

On the contrary, it's very descriptive: ''I am the far-away fire and the sword in the distance.'' That's exactly what *La insurrección solitaria* is: far-away fire and distant sword. The sword is a weapon and the fire is a living thing—two things that can be called completely dynamic. Not only that, but aggressive. And not only that, but in a certain moment destructive and constructive. Fire can serve to warm you, to give you life, but it can also be used to burn something. The sword can serve to defend your life; it can serve to end another life as well. And, of course, the fact that Marcela said it is discreetly hidden here. I quoted the speech of the woman but that incident in *El Quijote* when Marcela defends herself after Grisóstomo's suicide didn't interest me a great deal.

You know quite a bit about painting and the history of art. Which artists interest you the most?

Painting has always had an enormous influence on my poetry. As an example, let me tell you about two paintings in Paris that I saw in the Louvre. A painting by Lucas de Leiden called *Lot and His Daughters* appears in my poem "Kiss for Lot's Wife." The destroyed city in the painting, Sodom, "rhymes" with some sinking boats in the foreground: "Fireworks over Sodom./ Gold and crimson falling/ over the keel of the sinking city." I copied it directly—even the woman. I picture her left behind on the little bridge. My theory in the poem is that she didn't turn around out of some feminine curiosity, but that she left something profound in the city. And what's the only profound thing for a woman? A lover. It's not a bag of jewels. Also, a painting by Pieter Bruegel, *The Lepers*, has to do with the last part of my poem, "Two Murals: U.S.A."

Do you think that poem is a kind of painting of modern life in the manner of Baudelaire?

You mean like the painter in "Le peintre de la vie moderne?" Or when Baudelaire sends a letter to Huysman while he's writing "Spleen" that says: "I want to write a few poems in prose based on the great and famous work by Aloysius Bertrand called "Gaspard de la nuit" from *Histoires vermoulues et poudreuses du Moyen Age*? It wasn't really famous, because no one even knew that it had been published. It's like that time when you asked me: "Why didn't anyone in Spain notice when you published "Two Murals: U.S.A." in *Cuadernos Hispanoamericanos*?" In 1857 two books were published that were judged to be immoral, obscene, and pornographic: *Madame Bovary* and *Les fleurs du mal*. And both books, in spite of the fact that the authors weren't friends, were processed by the same man, who was very important in the government at the time. The authors were fined and the editions were confiscated. Flaubert and Baudelaire, even though they didn't know each other, were born in 1821.

What did you learn from Baudelaire about the relations between men and women?

Nothing, because he was never able to teach anything about that. He fell in love with Jeanne Duval and never fell in love with anyone else. And Chesterton maintains that he died a virgin. He fell in love with Jeanne Duval, a black woman, one afternoon when she was playing a bit part in some unimportant play. The only thing she said when she came on stage was, "Madame, dinner is served." Baudelaire fell in love with her and it was unrequited love. What can poor Baudelaire teach? He didn't know anything. The only thing he lived was the jealousy he felt concerning his mother and Aupick, her second husband after the death of his father—and, of course, the sordid, incomprehensible relation with the mulatto, Jeanne Duval. And that's the way he spent his life until it consumed him. He died very young, at the age of 46. But, yes, he's basic to my work. I don't know what I would have been without Baudelaire. I can't conceive of it. I don't know what my life would have been without the friendship of Charles Baudelaire. Because there are authors who are authors—for example, Joyce or Proust: I don't have anything to do with Proust, I'm only interested in the work itself—but with Baudelaire, it's Baudelaire himself I knew. My friendship is personal with him. This doesn't mean that his work lacks the literary quality of Proust's. But I identify with him as if he had been a friend of mine. I feel his suffering and I understand his decay and his weakness and his joy.

What other writers do you identify with in this same vital, personal sense?

Robert Burns, François Villon. With all the delinquents. Really, it's with the delinquent authors. In other words, with those who lead lives filled with remorse.

What's your greatest remorse?

Being born. No, no, no, I'm joking. Because I'm not guilty and, besides, that's from Calderón's *La vida es sueño*, when Segismundo says: "El delito mayor del hombre es haber nacido." [Man's greatest crime is having been born.] No. My greatest remorse is continuing to live. I'm not guilty for having been born. I was begotten. But continuing to live does depend on me. In other words, my remorse is not having the ability to be a suicide.

There are many kinds of suicides.

Of course. And the suicide who does not commit suicide but kills himself another way is worse. That's the suicide of a coward. The most concrete type takes his life at a determined moment. The suicide who takes his life little by little isn't worth anything. That kind of person has a double guilt: the basic guilt that would make him kill himself and the guilt for not killing himself. Crevel, Crosby—I have a devoted admiration for those who can do it, because I can't. It's more like watching a great acrobat leap, a trapeze artist, not a great poet, or a great musician, or a great sculptor or painter. These seem to me within my reach. But when I see one of those acrobats, someone filled with grace and strength . . . I would rather be the happy thing that *falls*. Rilke mentions it in the *Duino Elegies*. That's great! In complete harmony with nature. Like a piece of fruit. There's another suicide I enjoyed a great deal, the English actor George Sanders. He killed himself in Madrid. I was overjoyed when I read in *ABC* the news of his suicide and that they had found him in his hotel room. The note said, more or less: "I'm not going to blame anyone or make any speeches or try to investigate my suicide. I don't want to involve anyone. I'm committing suicide because I'm bored." Baudelaire's *ennui*. The boredom of living. But the interior condition of the suicide is something endowed with genius and not everyone can participate in it.

What do you mean, "endowed with genius"?

Who knows what they see that enables them to do it? Or who knows their unique penetration into reality? Who knows what dimension, what fourth or fifth dimension, allows them to lose their instinct for self-preservation—something that is completely vulgar. That's why the suicide is basically a genius.

Didn't Baudelaire also invent the concept of the flâneur*?*

Yes. He put it in a literary category. The *flâneur* existed before. But he gave it a name. He converted it from practice into theory. And that's important. When something is just practical, it isn't worth anything. But the moment practice is converted into theory, it becomes eternal.

What was that theory?

The *flâneur* walks with his hands like this, behind his back—similar to what we were talking about with Aloysius Bertrand. You asked me if I had wanted to put something about modern life in my poem, "Two Murals: U.S.A." Based on his experiences as a *flâneur*, Baudelaire wrote the "Parisian Scenes." It's all from the observations by the man of talent, the solitary intellectual as he moves through the city and *la foule*—the crowd. The same things later provoked in painting the great, falcon-like visions of the city painted by Pissarro.

"Fourmillante cité, cité pleine de rêves."

That's right. And that's the way Baudelaire was as a *flâneur.*

A hidden prince, traveling incognito. He carried his class with him.

Yes. Tremendously. When Baudelaire arrived in Belgium, he carried with him his manner of dress, his behavior, his coldness. He hated women, for example. He said, "La femme est naturelle, c'est-à-dire, abominable." Because he thought one shouldn't be natural, that one should be a dandy. That's why Pasternak says that our great poetry can no longer depend on the countryside—no matter how badly we would like to return to the countryside—ever since Baudelaire invented the poetry of the city. In other words, he invented dandyism and finished off nature. The world of poetry was converted into the "fourmillante cité." Baudelaire created that historical change of historic mentality. It was imposed on him. A genius receives a new category of the universe, a new way of seeing the universe, and must bear it—even if that way of seeing is painful. It would be a lot better to think about the countryside, the streams, the murmur of the water and the song of the birds. But it isn't necessarily what you discover. It's what you want to discover. It's imposed on you and sometimes it's fatal. Baudelaire was the victim of being Baudelaire.

Can you describe the genesis of your poem "Two Murals: U.S.A."?

That was in 1955 when I was working in the language laboratory in the Department of Romance Languages at UCLA. After that, I went to work in the Bank of America, because I didn't have a degree from a university and couldn't get a position as a professor of literature. What happened is that during those months when I went from Paris to Nicaragua, after having chosen to do my thesis on Chartres cathedral, my mother died. She was the one who had sent me money so I could study. That's when I fell into *somocismo*. But in 1955, when I was at a department store called Bullock's, I saw death enter—that woman in the poem, "the upcoming death." So I wrote down on a little card: "The woman I saw at Bullock's. Don't forget. Write a possible poem to be entitled 'Reflections on a Passerby'." And that's all I thought I was going to write. The first poem, "The Upcoming Death," begins with the quotation from Eliphaz the Temanite: "Then a spirit passed before my face . . . ." That's where I got the most important part of the poem. I'm referring to the part that talks not about the fear we already know, but the new fear, the one that doesn't scare, the fear like the green grass, the beautiful fear. It's the fear of the United States underneath all those things that look like paradises. This isn't the old terror that had its image and against which you could defend yourself. You can't defend yourself from the fear that is represented by little girls holding watering cans. First, there's a description of how people live in the United States. It's strange. How can fire escapes imprison you when they're supposed to be for escaping? Nevertheless, that's how it is. And the poem goes on with an image of the door at Bullock's that opened by itself. A double world of light and air enters. That's the problem with poetry: you see certain things inside you and before you—really clearly—and that's the way you write them. And later they say that you're obscure or that you try to be obscure. No. For me, all this is very clear.

And does the description continue in the second mural, "Here Stone Is Lacking"?

Yes. Take the title, for example. I was used to living in Europe where I was always bumping into some kind of stone: a cathedral, the public auctions, the stock exchange, the plaza. But in the United States it seems as though all the construction is built as if for a fair. And it's a country that's always under construction. Since I worked at the Bank of America at night, I used to listen to the machines that punched holes in the computer cards. Those machines were like cockroaches! And since I had to do a series of errands as an intermediary between the shipping companies and the customs house brokers, I wrote "Two Murals: U.S.A." going through the streets of Los Angeles. The murals were written, erased, corrected, and re-written all by memory.

Is there a spatial and temporal change in the last part of the poem?

Yes. Since the poem perceives the rupture of a cultural unity in the United States, there is a nostalgia for the Renaissance. It's the same nostalgia that appears in my poem "Pentecost Sunday in a Foreign Country."

What are the main differences between your poetry and Ernesto Cardenal's?

It's the difference between poetry that doesn't sacrifice itself to politics but, on the contrary, takes sides with a political party, and poetry that doesn't take sides with a political party *or* sacrifice itself to politics. In the absolutely traditional sense of François Villon and Robert Burns, my two masters, what I do is simply declare my individuality: what concerns me, what I like, what frightens me, what I don't like. *La insurrección solitaria* is a cultural, not a political insurrection. I have no ideas, no ideals, and no ideology. I only have thoughts. Thoughts that wither like flowers.

In your poem "Free Love," written in October 1979, you quote Revelations 21,1: "And I saw a new heaven and a new earth." Is the Nicaraguan Revolution a revelation in the Biblical sense?

I wrote that poem with the energy of the morning hours, when I used to travel by bus from Granada to Procampo in Managua where I had an office in the Ministry of Agrarian Reform. In the first place, I'm heliocentric. As long as the sun is up, I belong to the sun. When the sun goes down, I talk with the dying. That morning I was thinking about the Revolution. I had such a feeling of enthusiasm for the Revolution. Let's see . . . in July of '79 we got rid of him. August, September, then in October I wrote the poem. I loved Procampo. I had my "Tutankhamen's Tomb" where I wrote so much poetry. I was filled with creativity and power.

Do you consider yourself a patriot?

No, absolutely not. I have no civil patriotic sense. But I feel deeply attached to Nicaragua. It must be the genes of my parents. Pure biology. I feel I am in my element only when I'm here. Even though there's no time to do anything here in Nicaragua. In Nicaragua, you get up and just like that it's already getting dark. Against futility, I want to put utility. What a difference just one letter makes in someone's life. I did more in Los Angeles from 1954 to '64—in ten years—than in the twenty-two years I've lived in Nicaragua: all of *Allegro irato*, diaries, enormous chronicles about painting exhibits and visits to museums.

But how did you put up with life in Los Angeles?

It has been the same for me everywhere, because I've had to put up with myself, not with Los Angeles. I've been as happy in Paris as in Los Angeles, Madrid, or Granada. I mean, as happy or as unhappy. People ask things that don't make any sense to me: "How can you be in such and such a place when you've lived in Paris?" "But everywhere I've been, I'm unhappy," I tell them, "because I've been with myself." I don't like myself. So wherever I am, I'm displeased. And at the same time I'm happy, because even though I don't like myself I still have my ways of enjoying life. I don't need to live in Venice, Rome, New York, Paris, Granada, Niquinohomo, or Soria, like Antonio Machado. I don't think that Joyce was happy anywhere. He was Joyce, and he was miserable, and happy, because he had his work and that made him happy. And he was miserable because his work was the description of misery. His work was the retelling of misery, which was happiness for him.

Some people say that you're afraid to publish Allegro irato *because it doesn't reach the heights of* La insurrección solitaria.

They can say that for two reasons: either they know it isn't true or they are ignorant. In other words, either they do it as enemies, knowing it isn't so, or out of ignorance, possibly saying it in good faith and really believing it. But it isn't true. I never lowered the quality of my poetry. I couldn't include "Two Murals: U.S.A." in *La insurrección solitaria* and it's possible that the poem is better than *La insurrección solitaria*. That's also true of my poem "Heaven's Hell." Perhaps in poems like "Memory for the Year, Inconstant Wind" and "Portrait of a Lady with a Young Donor" from *Insurrección* there is only *strength*. But the other poems are rather austere. There's something in *La insurrección solitaria* that is broken in the later poems. They have that enthusiasm that is Greek frenzy as well. I believe "enthusiasm" corresponds to the nomenclature of Greek theater, the liberation from inhibitions and the identification with divinity: the delirium you achieve through music and dance!

When do you think you'll publish Allegro irato*?*

The problem is precisely the one with which Isadora Duncan begins her autobiography, *My Life*. I've loved my life. It gives me great delight to talk about it. But the problem was writing my life. I've enjoyed writing these poems and I have them over there in folders. But to make clean copies of them is so boring.

When you began to write your life, didn't you receive a great deal of critical support from José Coronel Urtecho?

If José Coronel hadn't existed, hardly anything would exist in Nicaragua. He taught us everything. He guided us. When we were fourteen, we would go to his house. The Jesuits who ran our high school gave us permission. José Coronel gave us the names of the authors we should read. He lent us important books. Thanks to him, I read André Gide as an adolescent. Coronel was very generous. He was never secretive concerning his knowledge. He was a simple man, but spoke with enthusiasm. It was not a magisterial attitude. He never said: "Here come my students, my disciples. I'm going to put on my toga." No. He was reading, perhaps. We appeared. He lifted his head, closed the book, put it to the side and said: "How are you? What have you been up to?" I remember when I read my poem "Paradise Regained" for the first time. I read it to two people: Joaquín Pasos and José Coronel. Joaquín Pasos burst into laughter at the end. I thought my poem was really bad. But later, when I was with Coronel next to the lake in Granada, I asked him: "*Poeta*, why did Joaquín burst into laughter?" "Ah," he told me, "poetry has that effect on him—so much so that when he started coming to my house and I read him Jorge Manrique and other classics from the Golden Age, he started to laugh. And I told him: 'Young man, please find another way to show your enthusiasm!' " Joaquín was divine. He was a poet—down to each cell in his body. Poetry made him die laughing from pure poetic enthusiasm. And, yes, José Coronel was very important to us all.

I imagine that José Coronel read the classics to you as well, didn't he?

Of course. Garcilaso, Quevedo, Lope, and Fray Luis de León have been basic for me in terms of the internal structure of my verse. And Góngora. As an innovator, he's probably the most interesting. The adventure of his "Soledades" is the greatest literary adventure of all. Then comes *Ulysses*. And the "Soledades" were written 300 years before. And also a lot of Cervantes' prose: the *Novelas ejemplares* above all. Cervantes is the master of the idiom. I've always believed that if you don't have an idiom, you don't even have thought. It's not the other way around. It's not that you express your thoughts with the idiom, but that the idiom makes you think.

What are the disadvantages of Spanish?

Perhaps there are some in the Spanish we speak today. But if we return to the Golden Age and the prose of Quevedo's *Los sueños*, Fray Luis de León's *Los nombres de Cristo*, and Cervantes' *Rinconete y Cortadillo*, all these are powerful. What I can't read is Spanish American prose. It seems really impoverished to me. It doesn't have any flavor. It's like passing sugar cane through the press a thousand times. But the prose of the classics has great flavor and great strength. *Lazarillo de Tormes*, for example, and *La Celestina*.

But doesn't the prose of Malcolm Lowry, especially in Under the Volcano, *interest you?*

Yes. It's dense and well-worked prose. But there is density that bores me, as in *Moby Dick*. I can't take it, in spite of the admiration my great Jack Kerouac had for that book and in spite of the fact that the book is important. It has good parts. But it's too heavy. *Under the Volcano* is never that way. Because there's so much work that each page is transparent. It's a goldsmith's transparency—luminous. It's the work of a supreme artist. For me, that great perfection isn't preciosity. It's not polishing from the outside toward the inside, but the perfection within brought out into the light. As in Proust. He isn't a a stylist. I don't believe in style.

You haven't said much about the poets of the Golden Age—Lope, for example.

Lope wrote his masterwork, *El Caballero de Olmedo,* near his his death. It is one of his most mature works—not the light entertainment he produced when he needed money or wanted to please the public. It's tighter in style, denser in thought, and darker in feeling. In Lope's work, when a gravedigger appears, one doesn't know if he is a gravedigger or a farmhand. One doesn't know whether he's burying seeds or burying the dead. Lope's ambiguity was something Calderón de la Barca never achieved. Calderón was extremely cold and intellectual. That's why the Germans liked him so much. In Lope, there's always a hazy emotive order that distinguishes him from the other Spanish playwrights: from Tirso, who was the exquisite expression, and from Calderón, who was the metaphysical expresssion of the Baroque. Lope always maintained his great vitality. He possessed what Nietzsche in a letter said that a writer should possess: culture and refinement but, at the same time, the basic impulsiveness of the instincts. When I saw the Hispanic American elite corrupted by Europe, I felt like a wildcat among them with all my Central American potency. And at the same time, in the same category. It's one thing to feel wild and be ignorant, and another to feel wild with just as much knowledge as they have. That's the difference Cortázar and Paz noticed in me. They were Hispanic Americans who belonged to the European elites. I was the Hispanic American who embraced everything they felt, saw, and knew—and I had remained savage.

Before we finish, you promised to play your guitar and sing.

If you insist . . . Federico García Lorca is the greatest poet that nature has produced in corporeal atoms, even though his premature death didn't allow him to develop his genius. But in this song of the dead gypsy, he expresses something that hadn't occurred to anyone. And that is that someone dies without anyone knowing who he is. In other words, without having any identification. The poem is called "Surprise."

It was dawn. No one
dared look at his eyes
open to the hard air.
There he was, dead in the street,
with a knife in his chest
and no one knew who he was.

Ernesto Cardenal

Ernesto Cardenal was born in 1925 in Granada, Nicar poetry, which has been translated into more than fi guages, embraces all the Americas and Cardenal acknowledges his debt to certain North American poets, especially Whitman, Pound, Williams, and Merton. In Cardenal's recent poetry, immediate social and political values enable the poet to take part in the collective process of a people attempting to realize their dream of self-determination. According to Cardenal, these ideals are best expressed in literature by means of what he calls "exteriorist" poetry, which he defines as "objective poetry: narrative and anecdotal, made of the elements of real life and concrete things, with proper names and precise details and exact data and numbers and facts and sayings . . . the only poetry that can express Latin American reality, reach the people, and be revolutionary."

Cardenal began his studies of literature in Managua and continued them in Mexico from 1942-1946. His literary works from this time, "La ciudad deshabitada" ("The Uninhabited City") and "El Conquistador," show the poetic influences of Pablo Neruda and Archibald MacLeish. After studying in New York for two years until 1949, Cardenal then spent two years in Europe, returning to Nicaragua at the end of 1950. In 1954, he actively participated in the "April Rebellion" against the elder Somoza. Cardenal incorporated this experience as well as a panorama of Central American history in his poem Hora cero *("Zero Hour"), first published in 1959.*

In 1957 Cardenal entered the Abbey of Gethsemani, where Thomas Merton was his Novice Master. After two years, Cardenal left the Abbey in Kentucky and went to Cuernavaca to study theology. In Mexico, he came into contact with an international group of writers that included some of the Beat poets and Margaret Randall, who was at that time getting the magazine El Corno Emplumado *underway.*

After continuing his religious studies and teaching at a seminary in Colombia for several years—it was during this time that he published the Epigramas *and wrote the* Salmos *(*Psalms*)—Cardenal returned to Nicaragua in 1965. He then established the Christian community called Solentiname on a lush tropical island that is part of an archipelago in Nicaragua's Great Lake. On August 15, 1965 Cardenal was ordained a priest. During the next ten years, while living in Solentiname, he produced many important works, including* El estrecho dudoso *(The Dubious Strait),*

Homenaje a los indios americanos (Homage to the American Indians) *and* En Cuba (In Cuba). *As a result of his experience and work with the campesinos of the archipelago, Cardenal published a valuable contribution to Liberation theology:* El Evangelio en Solentiname (The Gospel in Solentiname). *In 1977, after the Sandinista attack on the barracks at San Carlos and the wave of repression that followed, Cardenal was forced into exile and became a principal spokesman for the Frente Sandinista. When the dictator was overthrown on July 19, 1979, Ernesto Cardenal was named the first Minister of Culture in the history of Nicaragua.*

Since an extended interview was impossible because of Cardenal's many responsibilities as Minister of Culture, I have, with his permission, excerpted passages from some important speeches collected in the book Hacia una política cultural de la revolución popular sandinista (Towards a Definition of Culture and Politics in the Sandinista Revolution). *I have also used some fragments from an interview by Margaret Randall in* Christians in the Nicaraguan Revolution *and one by Ronald Christ that originally appeared in* Commonweal.

On pacificism and armed insurrection

There are Christians who are intransigent pacifists, mainly in the United States, and some are friends of mine. But their position is not in agreement with the Bible. The Bible blesses the sword of Holofernes when it is wielded by Judith. A North American Jesuit, who is a friend of mine and one of those intransigent pacifists, wrote me an open letter condemning my defense of the Sandinista struggle, saying that no principle, however high, could be worth the life of one single child. I replied that I agreed, but that the Sandinistas were fighting for thousands of lives of men and women, elders and children, who were being murdered every day, and that no principle of intransigent pacifism could be worth the life of even one of those children.

I wish that you could have seen or that you could see, if only in movies or photographs, the jubilance with which our people received the Sandinista combatants when they triumphantly entered Managua, and how the "muchachos," as they were lovingly called by the people, were received along their way. Many were children of fifteen years and even younger; there were also many young women. If only you could have seen how the people embraced those combatants. During the war many of the walls of the houses, which in those days were covered with slogans, had the following phrase with its biblical echo: "Blessed be the womb that bore a Sandinista combatant." This is because the combatants brought liberation and because they brought peace.

The Spanish writer Quevedo used to say that there is nothing worse for a people than tyranny, that it is worse than civil war, since it is civil war installed in power. We had almost a century of that type of civil war installed in power. The war by which we rid ourselves of it was not a civil war, as some falsely tried to portray it, but a war of liberation. *And* this war has brought us peace.[1]

We Christians find in recent Nicaraguan history an analogy to the message of Passover, that is to say, of death and resurrection. In this light, our theological reflections have deepened and our congregations have been revitalized. For Christians, participation in this Revolution has been an act of faith in Jesus Christ.[2]

On his participation in the "April Rebellion" of 1954—a failed attempt organized by ex-military officers to capture the elder Somoza and take power

One night the rebels entered Managua with a weapons cache and held a meeting—*we* held a meeting—with other people in the opposition. The plan was to go at midnight up to the presidential house, but some of the people in the group thought that there were too few people to carry out the plan. There was general disagreement. . . . I was appointed to follow Somoza, in order to be sure that Somoza was going to the presidential house. At that time, Somoza was at a party at the U.S. embassy. As I recall, another companion and I realized how dangerous our mission was—keeping an eye on the U.S. embassy, close enough so that we would know when Somoza left the party. When we saw him leave with his bodyguards, we followed, very closely, until we saw him enter the presidential house. Then we went to meet with the other members of our group, but we found that the plan was falling apart. Because there weren't enough men, the plan to assault the presidential house wasn't going to be carried out that night. The next day we met again, ready to fight; but, by noon, one of the rebels had been captured and tortured. Somoza found out about the conspiracy and gave orders to capture everyone. Some went into hiding, some sought asylum in embassies, some fled to the mountains, others were captured. All of the top leaders were arrested, tortured, and then murdered.[3]

On the arms race and nuclear war

In the case of the oppression of Nicaragua, the Sandinista Revolution had to resort to violence. It was the only option, and with it we were able to destroy the Somozist violence and achieve liberty and peace. In the case of nuclear violence, I don't believe that it should be opposed with more violence. I believe that in this case revolutionary behavior would be to oppose that violence with the action of the masses, the union of all people of good will, with civic protest, civil disobedience, and even pacifism. I hope my words reach my pacifist friend, Father Daniel Berrigan, so that he realizes that the Sandinistas make this distinction.

A certain moral imperative exists for all of us: we've got to try arms control and disarmament. We haven't even tried yet. We've lived for thirty years under nuclear terror. We must try this other form of international coexistence now that the nuclear holocaust is a real possibility.[4]

On the democratization of culture

Nicaragua is one of those countries recently liberated or in the process of liberation in Latin America, Africa, and Asia, where more than half of the world's population lives at the current time. The powerful social transformations in these countries embrace all fields of life.

The terrible problems of ignorance, disease, hunger, and misery can be solved only if our countries develop their economies in an historically short time and create new social structures. This is an eminently cultural matter as well. Our countries are promoting rapid change—not just of the traditional social structures, but also of cultural values and cultural needs. In order to leave economic underdevelopment behind, we've united cultural transformations with the idea of creating a society free of violence. All this is now being seriously threatened.

In Nicaragua, cultural liberation has been a part of the struggle for national liberation. This is why last January [1982] in Nicaragua on the anniversary of the birth of Rubén Darío, our great poet was proclaimed Hero of Cultural Independence and that day called Cultural Independence Day. The cultural (or anti-cultural) heritage left by a dictatorship imposed and maintained by the United States for half a century couldn't be more catastrophic. When the Revolution of July 19, 1979 triumphed, more than half the Nicaraguan population was illiterate. And for the dominating classes, the cultural metropolis was Miami.

Our Revolution is of the present and of the future; but it's also of the past. Our past has been revolutionized as well. In the first place, there was a resurrection of the dead (in the conscience of the people). Our history was suddenly changed. Our patrimony, which previously wasn't visible, became part of the present. National traditions flourished. Everything Nicaraguan was always united to the liberation movement, but liberation has been the precondition for these national traditions being transformed into a common good.

For Nicaragua's rich, diverse, and hitherto unknown *artesanía*, the Ministry of Culture has established various stores. The best works are exhibited in what we call the Gallery of the People's Arts, located in Managua in what used to be the branch office of a bank. We are looking after the artist's needs for cultural, economic, and political reasons, and consequently have developed our own non-capitalist means by suppressing intermediaries and giving artists government financing. It's a fact that in our countries, the penetration of capitalist civilization converts art into merchandise, strips it of its traditional functions, and changes it into a product for boutiques. Without their pottery, the campesinos eat from plastic plates; they no longer use natural fibers, and the artist depends increasingly on capital for his production. In Nicaragua, we're looking for an entirely different way. . . .

The culture of a society depends on the capacity of its members to develop themselves. If they don't have that ability, there can be no democratization of culture. No culture, and no democracy either.[5]

On the relationship between culture and society in the United States

Not too long ago, an article in the *Wall Street Journal* denounced the fact that in the United States works of art and literature had been converted into mere ornaments to be preserved as paper money or fiduciary funds. Society doesn't expect a Secretary of State to have any greater familiarity with history than what's necessary to pass a sixth-grade test. And the article added: "The United States has made business its culture, and culture its business." In Nicaragua, on the other hand, we've made Revolution our culture, and our culture a Revolution.[6]

President Reagan is taking away the food of the children in the United States to waste money on the ex-national guard of Somoza. The most dangerous thing for us and for the whole world is when interests of personal prestige are confused with those of the national security of the United States.[7]

On distinguishing between the people and the government of

the United States

We don't confuse the North American people with imperialism. In the Frente Sandinista's anthem, there's a part that says: "the *yanqui*, enemy of humanity." That's imperialism. But there is a certain spirit of the people in the United States that is with us. For example, there is all the great *yanqui* poetry that is being taught in the Ministry of Culture's Poetry Workshops to laborers, to people who live in the marginal barrios and indigenous communities, and to members of the armed forces as well.

The mystic of Nature, Henry David Thoreau, who was imprisoned because he refused to pay taxes in protest against the war with Mexico, is with us. And with us is that mystic of man's independence, Ralph Waldo Emerson. And with us is Whitman, the great mystic of democracy who dreamed of a paradise on American soil where all men and women were comrades, and who sang the fraternity of all humanity and peoples on earth. And with us also is Edgar Allan Poe, who studied at West Point, like Anastasio Somoza Debayle, but who, unlike Somoza Debayle, was expelled from West Point. Poe became disillusioned with the course taken by the civilization of the United States, which he disparagingly called *Appalachia*, and was found dead from drinking on a presidential election day in the United States. And with us are the spirits of Vachel Lindsay, poet of the small towns and prairies, that minstrel who traded poetry for food on the farms; and Carl Sandburg, the democratic bard, singer of the people of the great cities; and Robert Frost, the rural poet and singer of the simple people of New England; and Robinson Jeffers, singer of savage nature and enemy of the growth of North American civilization and precursor of all the ecologists; and Wallace Stevens, poet of irreality and the world of dreams, even though he was an official in an insurance company; and William Carlos Williams, a pediatrician and great poet of simple things, common language and a common North American reality; and Ezra Pound, the great singer against usury and all the aberrations of capitalism, even though he mistakenly believed in Mussolini; and Archibald MacLeish, who sang against the forgers of the North American economic empire; and Muriel Rukeyser, who sang in favor of the humble and against the war in Vietnam, a person who was radical when she was young and radical as an older woman when I knew her; and Thomas Merton, my Novice Master, the Trappist monk who wrote against nuclear terror and the arms race. All these figures I have just evoked are with the cause of the Nicaraguan people.

The great North American poets I've mentioned would really like the poetry of these new poets of the people, of the new Nicaragua, their brothers—Whitman would have called them comrades. And they would like the poetry of the comrades of the armed forces—the army, the police, the air force, and even State Security (the intelligence and counter-intelligence service).[8]

On the influence of North American literature

The principal influence on me, and one could say this of almost all the Nicaraguan literature of today, is the North American influence, from Whitman to the contemporary writers, the very newest. Ezra Pound has had a special influence on me. The technique of Pound has been the greatest lesson for me. *The Cantos*, yes, *The Cantos*, not the earlier poems. Almost all South American poetry has been influenced by Europe and especially by France, but Nicaragua has been influenced by North American poetry and now the influence of Nicaragua has extended to other countries, most notably to Cuba. Current revolutionary poetry from Cuba has been greatly influenced by Nicaraguan and North American poetry.

I have tried not to be difficult as Pound is, I have tried to use technique but in a way that can be understood by the people. Pound was not interested in being understood by them. . . .

Pound wrote much economic, social, and political poetry—principally economic—and I also have written quite a bit of economic poetry and some of my indigenous poems also have these themes. I have a poem about the Inca culture which is principally an economic poem about the socialism of the Incas. The poem is called "The Economy of Tahuantinsuyo." Tahuantinsuyo is the Quechua name of the Inca emperor. I also have other poems about the Mayas and they too touch greatly on the economic, political, and social themes.

I think that Pound's principal point, and this is *very* important for everyone to see today, is that the present capitalistic economy is an oppression of culture, of all aspects of man's life, and we ought to liberate ourselves from this oppression. He called it usury, the oppression of money, of the power of money, and I try also to treat this theme in historical poems of indigenous cultures as well as in some poems touching upon the theme of imperialism. In these poems I'm working with a preoccupation with the religious and mystical aspect of man's life and not just the economic. Speaking of the Incas, I say that their socialistic economy was an economy with religion. I am not interested in an economic liberation of man without the liberation of the *whole* man. . . .

José Coronel Urtecho told me that for Pound poetry was "poetry containing history"; and he told me that my poetry was "poetry containing history *and* wisdom." In reality, what I would have wanted to say is that my preoccupation—and that, also, of José Coronel Urtecho—is that of writing a poetry which serves others in communicating its meaning. It was in this sense that he understood the word "wisdom"—in the biblical sense of wisdom, in the sense the prophets gave to the word. For me, poetry is above all prophecy in the biblical sense of guidance.[9]

On the new popular poetry workshops in Nicaragua

The production of new poetry is amazing. In their poetry workshops, carpenters and construction workers learn techniques for writing good modern poetry and the results have been excellent—as good as was written before by the poets of our literary elite. There are poetry workshops in slums, in factories, in the army, and even among the police. I think Nicaragua is the only country in the world that publishes the poetry of the police.[10]

The Venezuelan writer Joaquín Marta Sosa has written the following about the workshops: "We can say that with the Sandinista Revolution, for the first time, the means of poetic production have been socialized. The people have started to become the owners of poetry in Nicaragua—not because they read more poetry in cheap editions, but because they produce poetry."

I recently read in *Time* magazine that books of poetry in the United States don't usually pile up at the cash registers. In Nicaragua, the editions of poetry published by the Ministry of Culture are all quickly sold. Our magazine *Poesía Libre*, which is dedicated solely to poetry and printed on kraft paper, is sold widely on a popular level. The first issues have been reprinted owing to high demand.[11]

On founding the community of Solentiname

I was ordained as a priest to come and establish the community here. It was Thomas Merton who gave me the idea. He had been a monk for twenty years and had written a great deal about that life but had become unhappy with monastic life. He was a famous contemplative writer, and during the early 1960s many young Americans went into Trappist monasteries because of him. Monasteries were multiplying in the U.S., in part because of Thomas Merton's books. And after twenty years, Merton was wanting out . . .

He knew it was a medieval, anachronistic lifestyle. Ridiculous. So he wanted to found a different kind of contemplative community outside the U.S. Merton was an enemy of the U.S., of Yankee civilization and everything it represented. He hated the bourgeois mentality most monks had. Despite being monks, they had reactionary politics. At first it was a shock for me to find out that he wanted to leave the life I was still so enthusiastic about. He told me that I was in my monastic honeymoon and that within a few years I too would find the life arid.

He thought this new community should be in Latin America. He wanted it to be in a poor place, with a peasant population, maybe with Indians. The original idea was to build it in the Andes. He talked about Ecuador, Colombia, Peru. So I said to him, why not Nicaragua? That's when he began to think seriously about the possibility of Nicaragua. First we considered the Río San Juan province. Coronel Urtecho, to whom I wrote, persuaded us not to go there because of the climate. You can't grow anything. Besides, the mosquitoes and the daily rain. . . . Another possibility was the island of Ometepe. Merton went through the paperwork with his superiors in Rome, or rather with the Vatican itself, so he could leave the congregation.

At first he thought about a monastery in Latin America, a sort of reformed Trappist Order—not wearing habits, for instance. He wrote to Pope John XXIII, who replied that he thought all Merton's suggestions were good, but that they should be implemented by a different order, not the Trappists. The Trappist Order should remain as it had been founded in the thirteenth century and innovations should be made by other orders. Merton read me the letter, and said: "The Pope is quite right. But what I want to do is leave here and found a new order."

Actually, his abbot went to Rome and convinced them not to allow him to leave. I imagine that the main reason was that he would create traumas for many youths, and for priests already trained by him. And he also made a lot of money for the monastery with his books.

I was the only novice he let know about the plan. He also told two other monks about it. He thought that the four of us would be the only ones to leave.

Next, I got sick. I had a continuous headache. They gave me all kinds of treatments but couldn't find a cure and after a while I couldn't keep up my responsibilities. I had to be exempted from more and more things: my work, choir, etc. And then a monk who had been a doctor before, and who was one of the ones involved in plans for the new monastery, said that I had to leave. For me this was a great shock. I went to see Merton almost in tears.

He cheered me up right away, and said it was a good thing. I was two months away from taking my vows. "But that's why it's a good thing. If you leave before making your vows then you won't have the problem I do being a monk from the Trappist Order. We are planning to leave anyway, now you can leave early."

Shortly after that an abbot from Cuernavaca came to visit. He was a good friend of Merton through correspondence. He was establishing a monastery that was quite progressive. This was before Vatican II. Both Merton and the abbot, Father Lemercier, had progressive ideas, which afterwards influenced the Vatican Council and the whole Church. . . . Merton spoke to him about my case. He said I could be accepted into his monastery as either a monk or a guest. I didn't want to go there as a monk, so I went as a guest.

In the meantime, Merton suggested I begin to study for the priesthood. The Church was still very clerical, so it would be important to be a priest in the kind of community we had in mind—especially if Merton was not allowed to leave and I had to establish the community. It would be difficult to exercise spiritual leadership if I wasn't a priest.

I studied for two years in Cuernavaca. While I was there Merton notified me that he had been denied permission to leave Gethsemani. He also informed us that he had been forbidden to write, so that letter would be his last. It was quite a shock. We had already made plans for his arrival in Mexico; his previous letters even dealt with the clothes he was going to wear when he arrived. He didn't want to dress in black like the Jehovah's Witnesses. He was going to come dressed as a sort of student. . . . We had everything ready. The plan was for him to stay in Mexico for about two months and then to go and find a place for the new community.

After his last letter, I continued my studies as he had advised me. Then, bit by bit, we started up a clandestine correspondence. At first he would send poems with a short note inside them. Then letters. In special circumstances, monks can write sealed letters that even the abbot cannot read. But as this exception became rather frequent, the abbot complained. Eventually the correspondence became normal again, although we still wrote a kind of code. For example, the plan for the community was known as Ometepe, after the place that we had chosen. The abbot didn't know the meaning of Ometepe.

I finished my studies for the priesthood in Colombia.

. . . .

When I was ordained, I already knew I'd be coming here, that I wouldn't be sent as a parish priest somewhere else. . . . I had visited Solentiname and knew it was the right place. I arranged with a bishop from this area to allow me to establish an order here. As soon as I was ordained, I came to San Carlos as an assistant to the parish priest in the village while I looked for land in Solentiname. Then José Coronel's wife, María Kautz, told me that there was an old man, a big landowner, who was selling one of his lands. When we came to see it, we got off the boat right here, on this point, and walked all around here and finally arrived at the church.

I hadn't known beforehand that the church of Solentiname was on his land. It was only half built and made of adobe. Later we covered and painted it, leaving the dirt floor. It seemed to me something . . . well, a very special coincidence. I was not looking for a church, but rather for the land, but on the land was the church of Solentiname. And besides, walking near the church you have the lake on both sides.

All this was wooded. It was like a jungle. You couldn't see much. The whole area is equivalent to about 100 square blocks. It was a very beautiful location, and I bought the land. The owner had a debt with the bank, and I simply took over the debt. It was 13,000 cordobas, which was about 2,000 dollars. I had half from a literary prize I had won, and I got the other half through collections among friends in Managua.

In Colombia I had talked about the plan with some friends who shared my ideas. Two of them left the seminary and the priesthood in order to come with me. Many of them did not believe it. Lots of people thought it was a lie that a priest was coming to Solentiname. When there weren't any priests in so many other places in Nicaragua, why would a priest come to Solentiname?[12]

. . . .

My contact with Tomás Borge and Carlos Fonseca [along with Silvio Mayorga, founders of the FSLN in 1961] was rather sporadic but continued over those years. First, in 1968 I got a letter from a guerrilla fighter who wanted to see me to talk about some things. I attended that meeting and talked at length with Tomás. He raised the question of the hierarchy in the Church, reactionary bishops, a Church that had to be changed. And he talked a lot about the struggle. I was in agreement with them, but I still thought that as a priest I could not take up arms.

This was when priests were becoming more and more progressive in Nicaragua. Uriel Molina from El Riguero had just come back to the country and we used to talk frequently. We felt that we had the same goals as the Sandinista Front, as the guerrillas, and that Christians and Marxists had to be allies. I continued to be in contact with the FSLN and had several meetings with Carlos Fonseca. I told him I agreed with everything, and supported their armed struggle. But as a priest I felt I could not kill. I even sent him a biography of Gandhi. He read and returned it, saying that the book had made him admire Gandhi a lot, but had made him more convinced of the need for armed struggle. Because in India, despite Gandhi, they were in terrible poverty, while in China, where there had been an armed revolution, the system had changed.

In 1971 I made a trip to Peru, where there was a progressive government, and afterwards I went to Chile and met with Allende. In Chile I met many Marxist priests. I even met a religious man who belonged to the Chilean revolutionary party, the MIR. He was armed and semi-underground because he could foresee a coup. When we met he said: "On television last night you said that Christians can be Marxists. There are some people who say that Christians, in order to be authentic Christians, have to be Marxists." I was convinced he was right. Later I went to Cuba, where I had a long conversation with Fidel Castro about the problem of Christianity in the revolution and Christianity and Marxism.

By then I had already made public statements in Managua declaring myself a socialist. I did not say I was Marxist; only socialist. Nevertheless, it was a great scandal. After returning from Cuba, I defended the Marxist revolution, although I still did not declare myself a Marxist in Nicaragua, because the whole Liberation theology movement had not yet emerged. However, there had been a gathering of theologians in Costa Rica where people had talked about Christianity and Marxism being compatible.

I met with Carlos Fonseca and Tomás Borge again in January 1975, after the attack on the house of Chema Castillo, which took place in December. [On December 27, 1974 an FSLN commando occupied the home of José Mario Castillo Quant, an associate of Somoza, who was giving a Christmas party. Hostages were held and the revolutionaries obtained the release of all political prisoners, a million dollars, and the publication of a lengthy manifesto.] They told me to go to the Russell Tribunal in Rome to denounce all the human rights violations that were taking place in Nicaragua. They told me that the FSLN was receiving very heavy blows, and peasant massacres were increasing in the guerrilla zone. The plan was to exterminate the peasantry in order to stop the guerrillas. So the Guard was killing people indiscriminately, men, women, and children. They were burning them alive on their farms, committing the worst atrocities in order to terrify them and force them to leave the area.

It was important to denounce all that. So they sent me to Rome in 1976. And you can say that by that time I was a member of the Sandinista Front, since I was carrying out a mission given to me by the Front. My integration was gradual. By that time my brother Fernando was in contact with the Front, studying it to see what the mentality was in the movement, but getting closer to it all the time. We were both collaborators.

Here in Solentiname, the young people who lived with me and the peasants from the area who were most identified with us were becoming increasingly revolutionary, fully revolutionary. We had been having discussions about Marxism for quite some time. We read Mao, all the speeches by Fidel that we could find, and had gradually come to support the Sandinista Front. The young men from the community were anxious to leave and go fight in the war. They began training for combat. Then Humberto Ortega [then a leading member of the FSLN, now one of the nine-member National Directorate, minister of defence, chief of staff of the army, and head of the national militia] sent me word from Costa Rica, saying that there would be an offensive in which Solentiname would take part, an action in the area of San Carlos.

Before that, Carlos Fonseca and Tomás Borge had suggested to me that I might be an executive member of the provisional government; they thought then that the Front would gain power soon. I said I wasn't convinced I should do it but would if they thought it best. I didn't really like the idea. This was an early plan. Afterwards, the Insurrectionist tendency decided to stage insurrections in various cities across the country and choose a provisional government. [The FSLN split into three tendencies in 1975: Prolonged People's War (GPP), Proletaria, and Insurrectionist or *Tercerista*. The tendencies united again in 1979. Cardenal and the Solentiname community belonged to the Insurrectionists.]

A number of respected Nicaraguans, who became known as *Los Doce* (The Twelve) formed a group in support of the FSLN in 1977. The first thing they did was write a public letter saying that the political crisis in Nicaragua could only be solved with the full participation of the FSLN. This group included well-known people: some in finance, others who were priests, and intellectuals like Sergio Ramírez. They carried out campaigns abroad in favor of the Sandinista Front. There were some meetings outside the country with all of them. The idea was that they would form part of a new government. My brother was a member. I had not been included, possibly because I had been making too much noise about being a Marxist and they were choosing a group of people who would not rock the boat, not provoke American aggression.

At Solentiname the threat was growing. I knew that at any time the National Guard could come to get me, put me in jail, and kill us all. And destroy everything. A few months after the boys began military training on the island, I had started to take the most important books off the island. The ones I couldn't take, I hid. But in the end, the Guard destroyed everything.[13]

. . . .

Later, our community entered the Sandinista Front to fight for liberation. As a result, Somoza's Guard destroyed the community's facilities: the great library we had, archelogical pieces, records, paintings, kilns for firing ceramic objects, everything. And because of us, the campesinos from the entire archipelago were repressed. And the Guard prohibited them from painting. And there was the case of the campesino girls who hid in the woods to paint. If a Guardsman found a painting in a hut, he'd slash it with a bayonet. Why am I telling you this? Because I want to give you an image of the cultural repression that existed under Somoza. Literature, music, and theater were repressed. This was because we had a literature of protest, songs with a political commitment, and popular street theater that served to agitate. And books were banned. At first, just the books that were considered most dangerous. But at the end all books were banned since all books were considered subversive.[14]

We are now starting to rebuild the community of Solentiname. It was not important before. Even though it was well known in many places, it was a modest experience. The only importance it had was that there we preached the Revolution as a Christian exigency. We prophesied, inspired by the Gospel, what has already happened. And some youths from my community gave their lives for that dream which has become a reality.[15]

On biblical themes, art, and Liberation theology

I'd like to refer specifically to a certain kind of primitive religious painting that the campesinos of Solentiname have been producing. One painter, a woman, painted a picture of a crucified Christ who was wearing the pants and shirt of a Nicaraguan campesino. This picture has been widely reproduced in Germany. In an interview, she said: "I painted Christ as one of us, a man, a *compañero*, a guerrilla who went to the mountains and was captured by the enemy." The Massacre of Innocents appears as a massacre of children and young people perpetrated by Somoza's Guard in a campesino village. The Expulsion of Merchants from the Temple is in a Catholic church of the new Nicaragua where Jesus with his campesino disciples are kicking out businessmen dressed in suits and ties. The Sermon on the Mount is Jesus speaking with a group of campesinos in front of the Lake of Nicaragua. The Resurrection is a Jesus with the face of Carlos Fonseca Amador, the founder of the Sandinista Front, rising from the tomb. Nicaraguans are a religious people. This is part of the popular culture. And in this kind of painting the biblical history is the same as the history of the people. They are within the history of the Kingdom. Jesus is one of us—a campesino and even a guerrilla. The death and resurrection of Jesus are the death and resurrection of the people.

Of course, these campesinos had already been exposed to theology (Liberation theology) during the time of Somoza, when, as I said, we discussed the Gospel. I published some of these commentaries in the book *El Evangelio en Solentiname.*[16]

. . . .

A short time ago, in Managua, the great theologian from Harvard University, Harvey Cox, protested U.S. intervention in El Salvador all day in front of the U.S. embassy. He later gave a talk on what he called the "theology of imperialism." According to him, this theology is being opposed by Islam in the Middle East and by Christians in Latin America. And North American Christians should show their solidarity with the struggles of their Christian brothers in Latin America and the rest of the world.

For these theologians of imperialism, theologians of destruction and death, the struggle for independence on the part of our peoples and their fight for wellbeing and peace are viewed as a conflict between two empires. Where can all this lead except to the holocaust?[17]

On the meaning of the word "revolution"

"Revolution" signifies a social change, and I relate it to its origin in Greek, *metanoia*, "change of attitude," traditionally translated as "conversion." This is what our Revolution has been—a great change, a conversion to love. While the word "revolution" does not sound right to many, "revolution" and "evolution" are closely related. Social revolutions are a continuation of the evolution of the planet and of the cosmos. Evolution happens in jumps and those jumps in human history are revolutions.

Each social step forward unites men more. The planet becomes ever smaller while humanity grows larger. This union of humanity will finally form a super-organism composed of conscious organisms in the way organisms are composed of cells, a super-consciousness made up of innumerable consciousnesses. The human individual will not lose his individuality in this super-organism, just as cells do not lose theirs in the organism, but will form part of a greater whole. . . .

I believe in the Kingdom of Heaven. But I believe that this kingdom will be established on earth, because Christ taught us to pray for the Kingdom to come to us—not for us to go to it. And I also believe in Heaven. Because it is enough to look up at night to see it: millions of stars with inhabited planets, with evolutions and revolutions such as ours, where the same super-organisms will also have to form. I think that the Kingdom of Heaven is on earth and the whole cosmos, the society of inhabited planets. And I believe in the resurrection of the dead in the Kingdom.

I'm asking the whole world to help the Revolution that is taking place in our country. Even though it is a small country, the Kingdom of Heaven should be established there, too. I'm telling you this since abroad there is a campaign of misinformation against us, and above all there is a conspiracy of silence. I'm asking for solidarity and help for the people of El Salvador who, in imitation of Christ, are offering their lives for justice. I'm asking for solidarity with that process of liberation and all liberation to come, in keeping with the law of the stars, which is the law of gravity, the law of attraction, the law of love.[18]

[1]Ernesto Cardenal, "Por una Cultura de la Paz" (Oct. 1980), *Hacia una política cultural de la revolución popular sandinista*, (Managua: Ministerio de Cultura, 1982), 190.

[2]Cardenal, "Por una Cultura de la Paz," 196.

[3]"Ernesto Cardenal y la Rebelión de Abril," *Ventana* 153 (7 April 1984), 2.

[4]Cardenal, "La Paz Mundial y la Revolución de Nicaragua" (May 1981), *Hacia una política cultural*, 209-210.

[5]Cardenal, "La Democratización de la Cultura" (April 1982), *Hacia una política cultural*, 252-256.

[6]Cardenal, "La Democratización de la Cultura," 256.

[7]Cardenal, "La Democratización de la Cultura," 264.

[8]Cardenal, "La Paz Mundial y la Revolución de Nicaragua," 213-215.

[9]Ronald Christ, "The Poetry of Useful Prophecy," *Commonweal*, vol. C, no. 8 (26 April 1974), 189-191.

[10]Cardenal, "Por una cultura de la Paz," 194.

[11]Cardenal, "La Democratización de la Cultura," 260-261.

[12]Margaret Randall, *Christians in the Nicaraguan Revolution*, trans. Mariana Valverde (Vancouver, B.C.: New Star Books, 1983), 41-43; 46-47.

[13]Randall, *Christians in the Nicaraguan Revolution*, 80-83.

[14]Cardenal, "La Democratización de la Cultura," 247-48.

[15]Cardenal, "Por una Cultura de la Paz," 196.

[16]Cardenal, "La Democratización de la Cultura," 259-60.

[17]Cardenal, "La Paz Mundial y la Revolución de Nicaragua," 209.

[18]Cardenal, "Por una Cultura de la Paz," 196-197.

The 1960s and '70s: A New Militancy

Sergio Ramírez

Nicaraguan poetry of the 1960s was marked by the political fervor throughout Latin America after the Cuban Revolution. It was at this time that a group of students at the National Autonomous University in León, Nicaragua, formed a cultural group called the Frente Ventana. Two writers, with the support of Provost Mariano Fiallos Gil, were particularly influential in the group's development: Fernando Gordillo (1940-1967) and Sergio Ramírez (b. 1942). *Through literary reunions and* Ventana *(Window)* magazine, the Frente Ventana tried to point the way to a new political awareness in accordance with the times. The group discussed the problems facing Nicaragua under the Somoza dictatorship and the "commitment" of the writer. It was, in other words, the cultural counterpart to the Frente Sandinista, founded at the same time with similar political and social ideals.

These concerns have continued to illuminate Sergio Ramírez's fiction. Tiempo de fulgor *(Time of Brilliance), a novel "filled with light" according to Nicaraguan critic Jorge Eduardo Arellano, is a portrait of nineteenth-century León with flashbacks to Nicaragua's colonial past. A novel recently published in English translation,* To Bury Our Fathers *(Readers International/Persea Books; originally published as* ¿Te dio miedo la sangre?*), begins in 1930 during the United States' occupation of Nicaragua. Ramírez also wrote the important biography of Nicaragua's "General of Free Men,"* El pensamiento vivo de Sandino *(The Living Thought of Sandino).*

In the introduction to El alba de oro *(The Golden Dawn), 1983, a collection of essays and speeches that reflects the last 150 years of Nicaraguan history, Ramírez speaks of the effect of his political involvement on his writing. His activities as a member of the important opposition group, The Twelve, during the last years of Somoza and as Nicaragua's current Vice President have kept him from writing fiction on a regular basis. "I am someone who longs for the creator's vocation and longs for the mystery of the blank page," he says. "But to say that the Revolution takes away time from my writing would be extremely unfair. On the contrary, the Revolution, made by my people with their uncompromising, humble resolve and with their weapons and dreams, is precisely what enables me to go on as a writer. It has given my work a form and a dimension that will make my future books possible."*

Could you define the role of the writer as "cultural worker" in Nicaragua at this time?

It seems to me that the invention, or at least the vitalization, of the term "cultural worker" has to do with the conditions of the country. I'm talking about the Nicaragua we received and the Nicaragua we're trying to rebuild. It's difficult to restrict the role of the writer to the act of merely writing. In the circumstances of the Revolution this would only be something passive. For writers and artists in general there is also a state of emergency, a state of alert.

When I'm asked this kind of question, I'm always reminded of a poem by Salomón de la Selva from *El soldado desconocido* (The Unknown Soldier), one of the most important books of our literature. On one of the battlefields of World War I, a group of soldiers talk about their former jobs: one was a bartender at a hotel in a port, another made barrels. "And what was I?", Salomón, who was a soldier in that war, asks himself. "Poet? I'd be ashamed to say it." Perhaps this sentence, this poem, is a kind of *ars poetica* of our commitment.

This is why I'd say two things in order to answer your question. First of all, we're at war and the writers are in the trenches, the place where we remember our job or try to exercise it in the middle of the battle. Because of the new, diverse, and multiple tasks imposed by the Revolution, some of us are even government figures. Secondly, there's something very important, even ethical, contained in the idea of "cultural worker." It has to do with the shame (as in the example from Salomón's poem) of admitting that one is only a poet or painter or novelist. This explains the origin of that militant term, which shows you what I mean by a position of participation, of the urgency to act beyond mere artistic execution. The artist must imprint a praxis on that execution.

All this has to do with what I was telling you at the beginning: the conditions of abandonment, backwardness, and poverty in which we found our country when we received it. And not just materially, but culturally as well. Many third-world writers and artists delude themselves in their declarations and programs by stating that one of their rights is to be subsidized so they can create. This is how they, as creators, perceive the division of labor. All this is like a stone hitting your teeth in Nicaragua right now. We're in a battle to the death with our past and with our enemies. We can't aspire, at least for the moment, to that division of labor. This is a country in which poets have had the traditional prestige of being "intelligent"—and intelligent for everything.

Now they've got to prove it. To be a cultural worker costs a lot for the person who wants to be just a writer: a job, a responsibility, commissions, evaluations, documents, bureaucratic meetings, party meetings, meetings that last late into the night.

I'm sure that among our writers there are some who still have time to create in the middle of the urgencies of this accelerated life. Many good poems and books of poems have been produced after the revolutionary triumph. It's possible. It all depends on the individual. The mechanisms of creation are complex. But I can tell you that up until now, there hasn't been a single short story or a single new novel written by those who could call themselves the old professional writers of prose—even though there were never very many of us.

In terms of how it has affected me—if it's not an overstatement to say that we writers are good at everything—I do believe that the same sensibility that serves me as a writer also enables me to be a leader of the Revolution. What's more, I would assert that my position as a writer—one who incorporates the people in his work, who speaks from the people, and who rejects the traditional perspective of the man of letters using the vernacular and popular customs (like an entomologist with a magnifying glass)—is an essential part of my political apprenticeship and my class formation.

Here there's a meeting point with men such as Daniel Ortega and Tomás Borge, whose sensibility as guerrillas and clandestine leaders flowed naturally into a literary sensibility. In the middle of this is something that we're all accustomed to calling love.

And during all those years of struggle when I stopped writing (I finished my last novel, *¿Te dio miedo la sangre?*, in 1975) and during the years of the Revolution I have enriched that sensibility a great deal. I now have a much more profound vision of the people of my country. Traveling through Nicaragua and speaking with the people in the countryside and the city, one discovers a great quarry, shades of language, images, figures, gestures, characters, experiences, and events. Seen in this way, the Revolution is first and foremost a great human event that completely transforms lives, creates multiple new histories, events, heroisms, villainies, happiness and sorrow. Submerged in this world, I've been preparing myself to be a better writer. And I'm ready to write my best works—I'm sure of that. I'd call this a period of preparation or accumulation of forces in silence, in order to use the language of the guerrilla—not just in terms of the stories and visions gathered in my memory and notes, but in terms of language as well. The Revolution is also a great verbal marathon and the position of a leader, if one is a writer at the same time, is a privileged one that enables a person to learn.

But, in addition, there's all that I've written in spite of myself. As a leader, I'm constantly called on to speak before very diverse audiences: factory workers, community people, campesino leaders, students, youth assemblies, professionals, academics. From these expositions and speeches during the course of three years, I've extracted a series of texts that have a political value because they have to do with the history of the country and Sandinism, with the ideological struggle, with the interpretation of culture in the context of the Revolution, with education and with the economy. I think they express me as a writer. I've revised these texts, and perhaps I'll publish a book that will be my testimony as an intellectual inside the Revolution, living it every day.

You've spoken about your inclinations as a writer and as a leader of the Revolution. Could you describe the founding of the Frente Ventana in León in the 1960s and its relation to the Sandinista Front for National Liberation?

I came to León to study law in May of 1959, and it was one of the turning points in my life. I came from a provincial background that was quite poor—I'm referring to the village where I was born—with a very limited knowledge of literature that I acquired in high school. I was also distant from the fight against the dictator, which had an intense center in León, a university city. Somoza García, the founder of the dictatorship, was executed here in 1956 by a poet named Rigoberto López Pérez and professors and students had been shaken by the repression that followed the death of the tyrant. Among these people were Carlos Fonseca and Tomás Borge. Just a few months before my arrival in León, Tomás had fled to Honduras after being released from jail owing to student pressure. Carlos Fonseca had returned from Moscow in December of 1957 and suffered imprisonment just for having taken that trip and writing his book, *Un Nicaragüense en Moscú* (A Nicaraguan in Moscow), which the students read clandestinely. He was also persecuted and sent into exile to Guatemala in April of 1959.

In the university, a strong opposition to the dictatorship was forged, one that contradicted the accommodating position of the traditional political parties. In these radical positions of the CUUN (Centro Universitario, University Center), the central student organization, were the first seeds of the political lines of the FSLN: the rejection of the Yankee involvement (the CUUN had prevented President Eisenhower's brother, Milton, from receiving an honorary doctorate granted to him by the university on the occasion of his visit to Nicaragua in 1958), the demand that democracy go beyond the simple representative formula as an alternative to the dictatorship, the plans for an agrarian reform and for the regaining of natural resources. The university was a sounding board for the country's reality and the daily repression of the campesinos who demanded the return of communal lands taken by the large landowners. Some of the dictatorship's harshest injustices were committed against the indigenous population of Subtiava, a part of León.

These were also the days of the Cuban revolution and its first definite measures. Pérez Jiménez had been killed in Venezuela, the war of liberation was being waged in Algeria, and the road that opened in the minds of the future founders of the FSLN in Nicaragua was that of the armed struggle as opposed to the electoral route. But in that year of 1959, the bourgeoisie also took up arms against the dictatorship. In June, classes were suspended during the invasion of Olama and Mollejones and an aerial deployment on the plains of Chontales and Boaco that was quickly defeated by the National Guard. There were open conspiracies against the Somoza dictatorship in Central America, Mexico, Venezuela, and Cuba, and that attempt was the frustrated result of those conspiracies. With what proved to be a more radical and firmer stance, another group of exiles was organized in Honduras to enter Nicaraguan territory from the north. Among those people was Carlos Fonseca. The Honduran army, in agreement with Somoza's, surprised the group in Chaparral, attacked it from a safe position, and dispersed it. Carlos Fonseca was presumed dead in this action in which he was wounded.

The events of Chaparral occurred during the first days of July, when classes had been started again, and these events produced great agitation in the streets and churches. Vendors from the market and the indigenous population from Subtiava joined the marching students. During one of these protests, on July 23, the National Guard opened fire on us. Four students were killed and more than seventy wounded. That massacre had an intense emotional effect on the city and on the country. For me, and many others of my generation, it was the point of no return. We were deeply and decidedly shaken. Two classmates, adolescents no different from me, were among the dead. It was my first direct experience with death and brutality. We would never be the same; after that blow we matured. Our eyes were opened to the true Nicaragua.

This was the generation of the autonomy of the university. Some of us were inexperienced greenhorns who had just entered the university. Others, including Fernando Gordillo, had arrived in 1958—the same year in which autonomy was achieved. At that time we developed a sense of unity that was generational and consolidated a political identity that led to the organization of the Frente Estudiantil Revolucionario (Revolutionary Student Front). The FER, as a leftist organization, began to dominate the political activities in the university by winning the elections for President of the CUUN. At almost the same time in Managua, the Juventud Patriótica (Patriotic Youth) emerged, and it was through both organizations that the FSLN received its revolutionary impetus.

In this climate, the literary group called the Frente Ventana was born. Fernando Gordillo and I organized it with the support of Mariano Fiallos Gil, an exceptional man who accepted his appointment as University Provost in 1957 under the condition that the university be granted autonomy. For four years, beginning in June of 1960, the literary group published the magazine of the same name.

The magazine and the group were born with the wounds of the massacre. We were repulsed by the dictatorship and had a militant conception of literature—not socialist realism or anything like that. But from the beginning we did reject the position that had reigned in Nicaragua up to that time in terms of artistic labor: the famous story of art for art's sake; the artist's sworn aversion to political contamination. At that time emerged a group that was the fundamental contradiction between our position and the position through which traditional literature hoped to renew itself. This group appeared in Managua and was called the Generación Traicionada (Betrayed Generation). It alleged a betrayal that was the same as that of the "angry young men" in England and the Beat Generation in the United States. Peyote protest and ragged, wandering poets opposed to the cement jungle and existential void of the great cities. We took a very clear ideological position, and in our rejection of what was nothing but the old dependence on foreign cultural models (however justifiable these models were in their own countries), we proposed political commitment. We spoke of the miners with silicosis in Siuna, the poor who lived in Acahualinca and other parts of Nicaragua and we tried to resolve this political position in artistic language. One could say that in literature and art these were already the positions of the recently created Frente Sandinista, which was nourished by the radicalized youth movement headed by our generation. In 1962 when Carlos Fonseca, who was living in hiding, secretly spoke with us in

León, he reminded us of the political importance that the Frente Ventana already had and of the need to maintain it.

Looking back on those years of literary and political agitation, one could say that they were a contribution—a link—in a period of definitions necessary to break with the past. We entered into a new commitment, a new form of artistic as well as political struggle. We were not, as we said at the time, the Betrayed Generation. We were the generation that didn't want to betray Nicaragua.

How did the bourgeoisie fail in the constitution of a cultural project in Nicaragua?

The most important characteristic of the Nicaraguan bourgeoisie's cultural attitude throughout history has been its desire to import a model. This can be seen in different contexts. The first bearers of federalism after Nicaragua's independence from Spain tried to implant a North American liberal model. When Zelaya took power in 1893, the same liberal model triumphed in Nicaragua after one century's delay. Zelaya represented a new class, the coffee growers, and finished off the old institutions, stripped the church of its economic privileges, and secularized the state. In addition, he was aware of the use of machinery, technology, the telegraph, electricity, trains, the need for the territorial unity of the country, education, and the spreading of technical skills to promote capitalist production.

That liberal project was frustrated by the brutal Yankee intervention of 1912, after the United States had made possible the triumph of the conservative counterrevolution in 1909. The Yankees didn't want Nicaragua to be a nation, and the conservatives imported at the time the worst and most evil of cultural models: foreign will applied to all orders of national life. It was as if they had imported the void itself and the country regressed many years in terms of poverty, illiteracy, backwardness of the campesinos. In short, it was a restoration of the thirty years of the conservatives in the nineteenth century—but much worse.

The United States didn't contribute anything to my country during those years: nothing of its technological progress, nothing of its universities, nothing of its capitalist culture. Rather, there was a merciless looting and a systematic corruption of the dominant groups that became more venal and cruel.

Somoza, who took power after the murder of Sandino and became a substitute for armed intervention, continued that process of submission, which demanded nothing in exchange for the country and, under the pretext of continental defense because of

World War II, the circle of unconditional submission closed. From then on reigned the ideology of Panamericanism, Yankee patronage as a providential blessing—both of which were values that had been introduced into the soul of the liberal and conservative castes. This admiration became more pronounced during the cotton boom at the beginning of the 1950s. The bourgeoisie sent its children to North American universities to receive the metropolitan consecration, speaking English became a letter of citizenship, Miami was a spiritual Mecca, and the importation of architectonic models (furniture, fashions, music, and love for the "American way of life") created an umbilical cord that even today cannot be cut.

So, what I'm telling you is that the bourgeoisie failed in the constitution of a cultural project in Nicaragua because it failed as a social class. It never thought of building anything inside the country, it never developed a national awareness, and Somocism took this spread-legs attitude to its climax. But beyond its own limits as a class, it also failed to develop its alternative, which was the transplanting of the Yankee cultural model for the country. For this reason its frustration became perpetual.

It was fortunate that Somocism was unable to consolidate a cultural model with an articulated ideology and with organic instruments. Its attitudes and cultural answers were always marginal and did not result in the institutionalization of the pretentious—though it did abuse the figure of Darío by lowering him to a provincial symbol celebrated in tacky literary contests and the crowning of muses in country clubs. This, I repeat, in the long run, was fortunate for the country since it would have been difficult to destroy a firmly entrenched Somocist cultural apparatus.

This is why it's important to see how a new revolutionary culture that began to emerge in the country during the 1960s had to make its way between two closed walls: a degenerating and obtuse Somocism as well as the traditional culture that is the literature and legacy of the Vanguardia, a group that emerged at the end of the 1920s. And at the end of this narrow passage, imperialism was cutting us off and blocking our path. The Ventana group began to break with all of this. Afterwards came the generation of Leonel Rugama, who took up arms to live a clandestine life without renouncing literature. Later, there was the Praxis group of painters, the Gradas group of poets and musicians who agitated with songs and poetry in the streets. This current grew stronger very quickly. After the revolutionary triumph, a victory that was the result of the participation of writers and artists as well, Somocist culture was swept away in a matter of hours. Those who have remained and assumed traditional or reactionary positions in the arts have become a simple minority.

We broke down these barriers and now we're strengthening a new culture. Its base is the popular force that had been on the outskirts of culture for so long. Now, well armed, we can face the task of breaking down the foreign domination that has blocked our path.

You speak about the obstacle at the end of the road. What effect has the foreign policy of the United States had on the cultural development of Nicaragua in the last two decades?

In the last two decades, as in previous decades, the United States played with the destiny of our country and tried in vain to denationalize us. It wanted to turn us all into spitting images of Adolfo Díaz and Somoza. Somoza and his court spoke English among themselves, a comical English from the high schools of the 1950s. The United States wanted to turn us into a branch of the Southern Command and bless us every so often with concerts by the U.S. Air Force band stationed in the canal zone. The United States wanted to give us the gift of tons of *Reader's Digest* magazines to make us thoroughly anti-Communist. But worse than that, they wanted to turn us into mediocre thinkers. Somoza is gone, but he left us a bourgeois elite that still thinks in English and is horrified by our bad-mannered treatment of the Yankees who still want to give us orders.

It could be that there is another United States, an immense country of simple people who are permanently manipulated, a country of politically aware people and lucid intellectuals. But this isn't the country we know. We only know the United States with the sharp claws that invaded us twice in this century, looted our forests and mines, gave us Somoza, Somoza's children, and failed in imposing Somoza's grandchildren on us. We know the United States of John Foster Dulles, General Eisenhower, and of Nixon, who were allies of Somoza, and we know the United States of Reagan, Haig, Kirkpatrick, and the Heritage Foundation that threatens to destroy us. This is our perception of the United States: we perceive cruelty and insidiousness, which are also cultural.

How can cultural dialogue between Nicaragua and the United States be improved?

Not through invitations from the Department of State to our artists (which almost no one would accept) nor by sending a pianist or a jazz group to Nicaragua every so often. It would have to be something much more profound. I'm talking about a radical change in attitude, which would mean an end to the deceit and the disinformation campaign that has brainwashed the North American public. The day that the average citizen of the United States realizes that in Nicaragua a poor and suffering people are struggling against a situation that one Yankee government after another left us, that we're trying to get rid of polio, illiteracy, unhealthy urban areas, that we're giving land to the campesinos—that's when true dialogue can begin. That's when the North American intellectuals can exercise their true influence on their people—the day when there's freedom of information in the United States.

I'm not saying that we shouldn't begin now. There's always something that can be done. But we ought to recognize the fact that the honest North American intellectuals are as defenseless as we are against this terrible machinery of propaganda.

Leonel Rugama

Even though he was only twenty years old when he died in 1970, Leonel Rugama had a deep effect on the recent course of Nicaraguan poetry. Before he became a celebrated hero of the Revolution and an exemplary model of a militant intellectual's conduct, his poem "The Earth Is a Satellite of the Moon" had been translated into a number of languages:

Apollo 2 cost more than Apollo 1
Apollo 1 cost a lot.

Apollo 3 cost more than Apollo 2
Apollo 2 cost more than Apollo 1
Apollo 1 cost a lot.

Apollo 4 cost more than Apollo 3
Apollo 3 cost more than Apollo 2
Apollo 2 cost more than Apollo 1
Apollo 1 cost a lot.

Apollo 8 cost a fortune but no one really cared
because the astronauts were Protestants
and read the Bible from the moon,
astonishing and making Christians happy everywhere.
And when they returned Pope Paul VI gave them his blessing.

Apollo 9 cost more than all the others together,
including Apollo 1 that cost a lot.

The great-grandparents of the people of Acahualinca
were less hungry than their grandparents.
The great-grandparents died of hunger.
The grandparents of the people of Acahualinca were
less hungry than their parents.
The grandparents died of hunger.
The parents of the people of Acahualinca were less
hungry than the children of the people there.
The parents died of hunger.
The people of Acahualinca are less hungry than the
children of the people there.
The children of the people of Acahualinca are not
born because of hunger

and hunger to be born, to die of hunger.
Blessed are the poor, for they shall inherit the moon.

In 1969, Leonel Rugama entered the university in León where he worked with the Frente Estudiantil Revolucionario and came into contact with Ricardo Morales Avilés, Omar Cabezas, and others who were involved with the Frente Sandinista. Rugama became a militant as the Sandinistas were recovering from a serious blow to their organization in 1967 when Somoza's soldiers raided a guerrilla training camp in Pancasán and killed many important Sandinista leaders.

The people who knew Rugama have a hard time reconciling his shyness and literary aspirations with his militancy, which obliged him to rob a bank, organize clandestine cells, and live underground. Someone apparently denounced Rugama's presence in Managua, and on January 15, 1970 no fewer than 200 National Guardsmen surrounded the house where Rugama shouted back, "Let your mother surrender!" Leonel Rugama died in combat along with two other compañeros.

On the tenth anniversary of Rugama's death, Commander Jaime Wheelock said, "We should not overlook the fact that Leonel was, above all, an intellectual—a poet of great esthetic quality. . . . But not all the intellectuals or the poets of Nicaragua . . . have had the luck, if it could be called that, to be poets within the Revolution or for the Revolution."

What follows is a homage to the poet by Commander Omar Cabezas, who received a 1982 Casa de las Américas prize for his testimonial book about his life as a guerrilla, La montaña es algo más que una inmensa estepa verde *(*Fire from the Mountain, *Crown). The tribute to Rugama was taken from the cultural magazine* Nicaráuac *6 (December 1981).*

Omar Cabezas

One of the most interesting aspects of Leonel Rugama's personality was his awareness of being as lasting as the wake behind a boat. In other words, he had a great awareness of his transitory nature. "I'm just passing through," he used to say. "I'm on my way, and while I go I make these poems. These are poems of no return." But the most beautiful and extraordinary thing about Leonel's personality is that during the brevity of his stay, of which he was fully aware, he always persisted in saying what had to be done. During that little piece of life he had as a man, he talked about what was most useful for everyone, not just one person. Leonel was always giving of himself to everyone and talking about Che. We used to meet at the university and discuss things, and I remember how Leonel would wrinkle his brow, get excited, clench his teeth, and say in an energetic tone with his hands and eyes: "You've got to be like Che! You've got to be like Che! Be like Che! Be like Che!" He said it with such firmness and sharpness, and with his eyes. He had eyes of honey, and he made fun of the girls, telling them his eyes were prettier. Then he would take off his glasses.

As I was leaving the university, going down some steps quickly, I kept thinking about what Leonel had said, as if it were on a tape: "Be like Che! Be like Che!" Leonel was aware that his life was going to be relatively short and he was ready to make an entire piece of art from the time he had. He was making a human work of art from his life. And for that reason, he was always uncompromising with himself, with us, and with everyone he had to be uncompromising with.

I don't know if it would be worthwhile in this homage to Leonel—after so many years and so many things have become clear—to make a confession. I was deeply envious of Leonel. I was envious of his great inner life. I mean, I felt that Leonel was intense. Leonel had just a short time. He was small, and his life was just a moment; but that moment, that life he made, had extraordinary depth, an incredibly rich content. Life was always spilling from his pores. You could see the life radiating from his eyes and you felt like getting inside those eyes, getting inside his brain and taking a look at what Leonel was thinking. That's what made me envious of Leonel, and I even told myself that someday I was going to have as much life as Leonel, that deep moment bathed in life that was Leonel. I don't know if he achieved it because his life was short or he was short or because he was a Sandinista revolutionary or because he was a poet. But one thing for sure is that what Leonel had was *life*, and that's what always made me envious—and I never told him.

Beltrán Morales

In Nicaragua, the 1960s produced a conflict of values between two principal groups of poets: the Frente Ventana in León and the Betrayed Generation in Managua. The Betrayed Generation, led by Roberto Cuadra (b. 1940) and Edwin Yllescas (b. 1941), then later joined for a short time by Beltrán Morales (b. 1945) and Iván Uriarte (b. 1942), essentially echoed the Beat poets and their bohemian lifestyle in the United States. The poets of the Betrayed Generation tended to be detached from the reality of their country, affirming in their manifestos: "We don't belong to any country, or any particular hemisphere; we are citizens of the planet." To which the Frente Ventana, in their cultural-political manifestos, would respond: "We are not the Betrayed Generation. We are the generation that will not betray Nicaragua." The members of the Betrayed Generation later recognized the naiveté of their position and rejected the false idealism of imported values, which had nothing to do with the growing crisis in Nicaragua.

Beltrán Morales has published numerous books of poetry, including Agua regia *(Royal Water), 1972;* Juicio final/Andante *(Final Judgment/Andante), 1976; and* Los nombres *(The Names), 1978. He also has written a book of literary criticism entitled,* Sin páginas amarillas, *1976, (Without Yellow Pages). The interview was conducted at the poet's home in July 1982.*

Could you explain the founding of the Betrayed Generation?

I made friends with Edwin Yllescas and Roberto Cuadra. But I didn't really belong to the Betrayed Generation. I identified more with the Frente Ventana, a parallel group that emerged in León in the '60s. There's something of a mystery concerning the founding of the Betrayed group, because it apparently took up the torch of the older writers—José Coronel Urtecho, Ernesto Cardenal, and Pablo Antonio Cuadra—but no one ever knew why the hell it was called the Betrayed Generation. Someone asked once: "But who has betrayed them?" I said: "Their girlfriends." But who knows? There isn't too much to say about the Betrayed Generation, except the scandal that some of Roberto Cuadra's poems caused. One of them was called "March." It began, "March. Accompaniment of waves. March is the month of the whores." And it went on like that.

Wasn't there some sort of conflict between the writers of the Frente Ventana and those of the Betrayed Generation?

There were arguments. Basically, they were political arguments. One could say that the writers of the Betrayed Generation were anti-esthetes and those of the Frente Ventana were socially oriented. For example, the Betrayed Generation quoted a line by Joaquín Pasos that says: "We are a vegetation of blood . . . We are the orchid of the steel." The Frente Ventana also used a poem by Joaquín Pasos as a banner—"The Indian Woman Who Collapsed in the Market." Joaquín Pasos was useful for the two bands.

What do the poets of the '60s owe to Carlos Martínez Rivas?

We lost a great deal with Carlos and we owe him a great deal, in the vital sense and in the literary sense. He doesn't have a single thought that isn't literary. But it's literature vitally understood.

Everyone seems to use the adjective "vital" when they talk about Carlos Martínez's poetry. In what sense is it "vital"?

The word "vital" is irremediably associated with a bad word, which is "life." When one thinks about Carlos, one thinks immediately about life. It's strange, because whoever reads Nicaraguan literature will never form a clear idea about the horror that Nicaragua really was. And whoever reads the work of Carlos Martínez isn't going to encounter that horror either, precisely because the work is literary. One doesn't realize how horrible life is from his work. Perhaps when we say that his poetry is vital we're really making a strictly literary category. When we say something is "vital" we understand it to be supercharged with life. Perhaps that's what we're referring to. But it's still a literary category. Breton said something very interesting: "Life and what is written are two different things." Carlos Martínez Rivas and life are two completely different things. We would also have to classify, for example, the category of poverty. What Carlos has lived is a kind of poverty. But it's not poverty.

I don't understand exactly what you mean.

The poverty of Carlos Martínez is like the line by the Cuban poet Lezama Lima: "I will seclude myself in the fear of a wall covered with elegant poverty." Carlos has suffered an "elegant poverty." He has never been abandoned by his upper-class friends who pamper him. What I'm telling you is that his suffering, in the economic sense, has been something very relative. It isn't "the whole pain" as Joaquín Pasos would have said. I think we all tend to exaggerate the genius of Carlos Martínez because in certain ways we would all like to be him. I've come to believe that even though we're in love with Carlos Martínez's bohemian lifestyle, the true poet is Ernesto Cardenal and not Carlos Martínez. I mean deep down. Carlos Martínez is someone with only one book—*La insurrección solitaria*. That just can't be. The career of a poet is like any other career with a sequence—something Carlos doesn't have. You can follow Ernesto Cardenal step by step through his work, and you don't necessarily have to refer to Ernesto as a person. I don't mean by this that Carlos doesn't have a body of work to back him up, just that it's fragmentary.

Did poetry from the United States have a very large influence on the poetry of your generation?

The anthology of North American poetry published by José Coronel Urtecho and Ernesto Cardenal was the Bible for two generations. But I was never too enthusiastic about it, perhaps because, as a friend once said, "We're under the poetic dollar, poet!"

What about the great poets of Latin America such as Neruda?

Cardenal has never been a friend of Neruda. That's the schooling we have received: a virulent hatred of Neruda for political reasons. Don't forget that even though we've had a revolution here, the older writers have been changing little by little. I remember, as late as 1965, Coronel Urtecho telling me: "It's incredible! That Nicolás Guillén and Alejo Carpentier in the service of Fidel Castro. Even though I'm for Somoza, I don't sing his cruelty." But everything has changed.

The political position of Pablo Antonio Cuadra has been more or less constant, hasn't it?

Pablo Antonio was imprisoned. When was Coronel Urtecho imprisoned? Pablo Antonio was put in jail in 1956 when old Somoza was executed. Carlos Fonseca, founder of the Frente Sandinista, told me that he was in the same cell where Pablo Antonio had been and that Pablo Antonio had written on the wall: "Here was imprisoned a free man." Pablo Antonio has been constant and faithful to a bourgeois democratic tradition.

Ricardo Morales Avilés

Ricardo Morales Avilés was born in Diriamba, Nicaragua, in 1939. After spending nine years in Mexico, he returned to Nicaragua in 1967 and joined the Frente Sandinista. In 1968 he was arrested, imprisoned, and tortured. During this time he wrote a number of poems, including "Brief Letter to My Wife":

If they kill me, I want them to know that I lived
in the struggle for life and humanity.
A world of all, for all.

If they kill me, a red rose
shaped like my heart
is the love I leave you.

If they kill me, it makes no difference.
I won't see the corn growing alongside the roads
or the bare feet on soft paths.
But I'll know that it's all there.

If they kill me, it doesn't matter.
Our cause will live on.
Others will continue the struggle.

The future is bright.

After he was released from jail, Ricardo Morales Avilés became part of the Sandinista National Directorate as the main ideologue in 1969. His most important writings were collected in 1974, a year after he died in combat in Nandaime. This book, El pensamiento vivo de Ricardo Morales Avilés *(The Living Thought of Ricardo Morales Avilés), contains the official political, military, and cultural position of the Frente Sandinista during the final years of its struggle to overthrow the Somoza dictatorship.*

In one of the chapters, "On the Revolutionary Militancy of Intellectuals," Morales Avilés analyzes Nicaraguan culture from a Marxist viewpoint. He finds a great deal to criticize in the reactionary stance of many writers associated with the Vanguardia movement, which is not surprising, given the Vanguardistas' intellectual and moral support of Somoza. But Morales Avilés also disagrees with Ernesto Cardenal's utopian, pacifist, communal lifestyle on Solentiname as having nothing to do with "scientific socialism" and the armed struggle against imperialism.

Excerpt from "On the Revolutionary Militancy of Intellectuals"

Intellectuals either produce and renew culture according to the taste and acceptance of the bourgeoisie and in the service of its domination, or they use the forms and means of culture as a revolutionary weapon at the service of the people. The question is this: will the intellectual perform a cultural function directed toward the people, or concede his position to the bourgeoisie and imperialism? For the revolutionary intellectual, the cultural battle is the battle for a new society . . . free from bourgeois interests. . . . The intellectual's role in this revolutionary struggle surpasses the merely cultural and esthetic in order to penetrate more profound concerns, such as the struggle for a society of free people working with the common means of production and making collective, conscientious use of all individual forces to guarantee everyone organized social satisfaction as well as the material conditions for a happy life.

It is an illusion to think that culture has nothing to do with revolutionary struggle—or is above it. Whoever thinks that way should consider the fact that revolutionary struggle, together with the history of the people . . . , is the praxis that generates conditions necessary for inexhaustible cultural creativity and unending human development. The cultural struggle cannot rest above the revolutionary struggle, nor lie parallel to it; the cultural struggle is an integral part, one front, of the revolutionary struggle. How can one talk about culture, national culture, creativity and development, goods and human cultural values, and personal realizations, when we face the everyday, concrete struggle in the streets, the countryside, the factories, the haciendas, the universities, and high schools? Given the current situation of the people, the fact that a prodigious literature can exist, esthetically speaking, in no way changes the reality of exploitation, hunger, illiteracy, and misery.

Now that the people have undertaken a political-military struggle for their own liberation, culture and cultural production have taken on a new meaning. To create means to focus on ideas that will crystallize the will of the people to fight. Doing intellectual work means uniting with the people's movement and struggle . . . and the intellectual's migration toward the people—which literally means going to the campesinos and workers, going to the proletariat—is the crux of the matter. . . . We must go to the past and present history of the people—rediscover the people.

I am not saying that previously intellectuals never moved toward the people or that intellectuals did not denounce the people's economic, political, and social conditions through literary works, essays, and scientific or political publications. That is not the case. But I am also not talking about the endearingly bitter substance of Joaquín Pasos' work, or the idyllic evocation of the campesino (the invocation of a devoured kingdom) in the work of Pablo Antonio Cuadra . . . nor the influence of José Coronel Urtecho, whose impact on the esthetic and innovative concerns of the Vanguardia poets is not entirely innocent, historically and politically speaking. Just as the expositions and prizes given by Esso, and the grants and travel-scholarships given to students, intellectuals, and artists by imperialism are not wholly innocent. The revolutionary intellectual must remain alert and militant in the face of imperialist support. He must expose the models that imperialism wants to impose and that students and some intellectuals unconsciously obey. . . . He must sharpen his critical sense in order to distinguish in the ideological manifestations all that tends to justify and maintain bourgeois domination. The reactionary stance of José Coronel Urtecho and the conciliatory humanism of Pablo Antonio Cuadra have the same structural and historical identity and the same end: to justify and to lay the foundation for domination by the bourgeois class. These poets try to present the ideals of the bourgeoisie as the ideals of all the people. They try to dominate the people like a government . . . , ignoring class struggle by talking about the interests of all humanity, pretending that people do not belong, except theoretically, to any social class. . . .

Thinking that literature and art are for an elite, and believing that the popular masses are incapable of understanding and appreciating art, is thinking with the individualistic mentality of the capitalist—me first, and *only* me. This attitude ignores the worker's ability to invent and to assimilate . . . ; it also ignores the fact that lack of interest on the part of the masses results from the structure of capitalistic social relations. . . . The realization of the individual must be the realization of each and every person. . . .

We appreciate more than anyone the kind of criticism that would defeat capitalism and imperialism; but we have to say to Father Ernesto Cardenal that the struggle against imperialism leads to scientific socialism and that experiences like Solentiname, despite their sincerity, the honesty and good intentions of men like him, are used by imperialism for the construction of illusions. This is why people do not need Solentiname today. Instead, we need to fight against Yankee imperialism, the bourgeois oligarchy, Somoza and his followers. It is important to assert this because positions close to revolutionary positions can be transformed and developed. . . .

Revolutionary intellectuals must organize and integrate themselves into the organized revolutionary movement. The revolutionary organization directs and coordinates the revolutionary struggle in its different levels and forms. In this way, the organization unites the cultural efforts of the intellectuals with the will of the people to liberate themselves. Through organization, ideas acquire a material force that cannot be contained.

To the history of revolutionary struggle and cultural efforts, the Frente Sandinista contributes the organizing of the intellectual practice of learning by making it a force that seeks to clarify our social and political reality and to help establish the popular revolutionary movement. Thus, the work of Fernando Gordillo must be understood as part of the organized cultural front that is organically related to the revolutionary movement. His literary work is committed along with his political and revolutionary struggles. . . . Now that the FSLN has consolidated itself—and its ability to organize along with its strategic revolutionary line have been established by means of a rich experience illuminated by science—there is a guarantee that what the Frente Sandinista represents can be developed and used to oppose the line followed by the Betrayed Generation. That attitude and thought, that ideology and politics, will only disappear when the bourgeois class and the social relations sustaining it disappear. . . . In our country, the armed struggle has been established as the primary means to achieve liberation and to take power. This implies that the intellectual must not only wield the weapons of criticism but must take up arms to fully assume his role in the revolutionary struggle. This is the path that intellectuals like Leonel Rugama have followed. Only through organized revolutionary militancy can intellectuals achieve a rational understanding of the progress and ends of the revolutionary movement, and so conscientiously participate in the transformation of the world. . . .

After the Revolution

Daisy Zamora

Daisy Zamora, combatant, poet and psychologist, was formerly the Vice Minister of Culture in Nicaragua. During the Final Offensive of the Frente Sandinista, she planned the programs for the clandestine radio station, Radio Sandino. Immediately after the triumph of the Revolution, she helped establish Nicaragua's first Ministry of Culture.

Initially, it was difficult for her to become intimately involved in the revolutionary process. In Margaret Randall's excellent book, Sandino's Daughters *(Vancouver, B.C.: New Star Books, 1981), Daisy Zamora speaks of having to overcome certain factors related to her upper-class background: "It wasn't until I left home completely, threw myself into the struggle full-time and went to fight alongside the other comrades, that I got over the feelings I had."*

Daisy Zamora's first book of poems, La violenta espuma *(The Violent Surf), collects work written during the decade 1968-78. The book is already in its second edition and Sergio Ramírez has praised its "creative authenticity."*

The interview took place in her office at the Ministry of Culture in July 1982.

Could you define the writer's role as a "cultural worker"? Isn't it a concept that evolved here after the Revolution?

I believe we've tried to give an organized response to that question through the Sandinista Association of Cultural Workers (ASTC). This is what we're working on now. Since we are living the transcendental historical moment of the Revolution, a writer can't stay on the sidelines of life. We've said many times that we believe the Revolution is the most important cultural fact in the history of Nicaragua. Logically, the writer should be involved in this experience. For myself, however, I haven't even had time to respond to that concern, because ever since July 19, 1979, when I was told that we had to put together a Ministry of Culture, I've been involved in the project. At that time, there were only five of us to give shape to this project of the Revolution, which has consumed all my energy.

What were the main difficulties?

I think the main difficulty was in finding ourselves. What would a Ministry of Culture be in the Revolution? Because, even though we were generally clear about the importance of culture, we didn't know how to give it a concrete form. It was like talking about the creation of a world—with no point of departure. In other words, the only starting point for us was the new reality of Nicaragua. We couldn't refer to the past, and that was the hardest part. It was a new reality and we had to create an entire project with hardly any direction or orientation because at the time we were told, "Let's see what you create." Of course, the first thing we did was investigate some institutions of the past and repeatedly refer to what had been written by the Sandinista leadership concerning the importance of cultural work. Above all, to the work of Ricardo Morales Avilés.

To The Living Thought of Ricardo Morales Avilés*?*

Yes. I remember that at the beginning people rained down on us from all over the country. People came with their guitars and all their instruments; people came who told us they were sculptors, writers, painters, all associating themselves with us because they were artists. But this Ministry itself was really chaotic. First of all, had you been here in those days, you would have seen that this place had been totally ripped apart by the people who took it over: it was a symbol of their revenge because the house had belonged to Somoza. Secondly, we didn't have desks or chairs or typewriters, and we all went around in our uniforms, not even knowing who everybody was. It was a tremendous mess around here. There, under those trees, would be groups of people who got together to talk or to play music.

It was a kind of spontaneous support.

Yes, but without any coherence. In other words, everyone was here waiting for us to tell them how they were going to work. Artists had come from all over the country and from all the fronts of the war. They sent us people just because it said on their identification card "I like to paint" or "I like to play the guitar". They were told: "To the Ministry of Culture!" Then it occurred to us to organize brigades in which we distributed all the people. That was the first job of the Ministry of Culture: Cultural Brigades. And we went out with them all over the country with the object of undertaking a campaign of direct information that would reach the people. We wanted to explain to them that there was a Ministry of

Culture and that it had been created with the birth of the Revolution. We said that culture was an integral part of the Revolution. While we were giving them all this information, we were also there to celebrate the triumph of the Revolution. After that earlier experience, when we went to the majority of the cities and villages in the country, the first program of the Ministry emerged: the cultural centers. Since people had already started coming to us and saying: "Well, you came here to talk about the Ministry of Culture. We already have a house in our village, and that can be our cultural center." That's how the idea was born for a program that now has disseminated cultural centers throughout the country. They are very important in that they support the increasing mass movement of Nicaraguan artisans, especially young people. Strangely enough—not in the pejorative sense, but in the sense of surprise or admiration—it has also affected the Nicaraguan campesinos a great deal. For example, in the rural sector, there is a very strong theater movement.

And the Festival of Corn?

Yes. The Festival was a program of the Ministry. It was a graphic synthesis of what we believe cultural work is in the Revolution. The program or the cultural centers, for example, had a really direct projection toward the community, a communal line of development concerned with rescuing the traditional festivals and supporting them. The Festival of Corn was extraordinary. The United States had just cut a large loan that was going to be used to purchase wheat in order to combat the scarcity of bread in the country. When this situation became clear, the Ministry of Internal Commerce called us and told us how important it was to get the message to the people that we were going to be without bread but that this was no reason to have a negative reaction. That's where the idea for the Festival of Corn came from. We looked up some of the work of researchers who had investigated this topic, like Dr. Dávila Bolaños who was murdered in Estelí by the National Guard. And we rescued from the past a Meso-american legend of Xilónem, the goddess of corn. Of the many legends about the birth of corn, this one told how, during a long drought when the people were dying of hunger, a Mayan princess sacrificed herself for her people. That's how we advertised the event: Xilónem returns after centuries to rescue her people from hunger. Immediately there was a massive response. Festivals were organized in the different provinces of Nicaragua in which anyone who knew how to make any food, drink, or dessert from corn could participate. We established seven different categories of food and advertised the event through the cultural centers and the popular organizations. The people who won the contests in the festivals in the provinces participated in the national Festival that was held in Monimbó. It was an experience that gave us an integrated panorama of what our cultural work meant. In the national Festival, one category was only tortillas. I talked to the woman who won and was recognized as the best maker of tortillas in the country. She told me how happy she was that she had realized that she was a keeper of the cultural tradition of her people. She said, "All my life I've been a cook, compañera. And I didn't realize until now that my work was important because now we are politically aware." She was truly proud of being a cook and of being a part of the people who have preserved a Nicaraguan tradition. We saved eighty-one different recipes for corn dishes that were on the verge of disappearing. As a result of the Xilónem Festival we published a recipe book that was distributed to the people. And what's more, everyone understood the message clearly. People told us, "Well, before we had to make contact bombs to defend ourselves against aggression. Now we're going to eat corn and tamales and tortillas and so what if there isn't any bread." It was an extraordinary experience for us. We repeated the idea in December when we had big foreign currency problems. Christmas here is a traditional festival that is very popular. We sent out a request to all the artisans of the country to participate in making toys for children. It was organized in record time and set up near the July 19 Plaza. It was called the Festival of the Piñata. The artisans came from all parts of Nicaragua to the festival with their toys and the people succeeded in filling the gap that we were going to have. There were toys for all the children at prices that were much more reasonable for the people. And besides that, the products were made in Nicaragua. The people have had the ability and the creativity to give answers like these in difficult moments.

Changing the subject a little, how do you explain the increase in the number of women writing poetry in Nicaragua today?

I don't think that it was something that happened instantaneously, but developed as women became more and more involved in the revolutionary process, starting quite a way back. During the war of liberation, the participation of women was decisive. I think this phenomenon, which is a result of the Nicaraguan woman's political awareness, has manifested itself in many fields—not just in literature.

How can the cultural dialogue between the United States and Nicaragua be increased?

I would ask: ''How can it be initiated?'' It seems to me that the idea of believing we can begin some dialogue with the government is a little outside our reality. But, yes, we still have a lot of hope in the more advanced sectors of the North American people—these are precisely the people we want to reach. One route is direct exchange between American and Nicaraguan intellectuals. I'm telling you all this based on my personal experience with the American Embassy. I spoke a couple of times with the ambassador, and there isn't any interest in initiating real exchange, apart from some jazz and dance groups they send us. I don't see any genuine interest in establishing any deep and direct ties that really form bridges between the two cultures. It doesn't exist. And I've been told that they have a very small budget for cultural activities of this kind. The official route really seems closed. With a great deal of creativity, we have to look for ways to establish direct ties. We also have to think of how people like you, who are familiar with Nicaraguan reality, can help us build bridges of communication. We're interested in sending representatives to several cities and universities in the United States so that they can explain to the most politically aware sectors something about the reality that all of Latin America represents—not just Nicaragua.

Rosario Murillo, Guillermo Rothschuh Villanueva, Eduardo Galeano, Francisco de Asís Fernández, and Juan Gelman

A discussion entitled "Entre la Libertad y el Miedo" (Between Freedom and Fear) was published in the March 7, 1981 issue of Ventana, the cultural supplement to Barricada, *the Frente Sandinista's official newspaper. Organized by several members of* Ventana*'s editorial staff, including Rosario Murillo, Guillermo Rothschuh Villanueva, and Francisco de Asís Fernández, the conversation also involved the well-known Uruguayan author of* The Open Veins of Latin America, *Eduardo Galeano, and the Argentine poet, Juan Gelman, whose* Hacia el sur *(Heading South) was recently published in Mexico. What follows is an excerpt from this fascinating inside look at cultural problems within the context of the Nicaraguan Revolution and revolutionary experiences in general.*

The discussion begins with the controversial subject of the poetry workshops organized by Mayra Jiménez, under the auspices of the Nicaraguan Ministry of Culture headed by Ernesto Cardenal. In this conversation, the fear that a single poetic language (promoted by an official organization) was being imposed on young writers surfaces repeatedly. In Nicaragua, where standards of excellence for poetry are very high, mere imitation of a certain style of writing is unacceptable.

In his book Pedagogy of the Oppressed *Paolo Freire discusses the dangers of the "banking" concept of education in oppressive societies where students are depositories and the teacher is depositor. Freire goes on to say that "the revolutionary society which practices banking education is either misguided or mistrusting of men." It is precisely between the parentheses of fear and freedom—fear of having one's ideas challenged in the context of the revolution and the freedom to realize new ideas—that the cultural revolution in Nicaragua is defining itself.*

A year after the Ventana *discussion, three ex-members of the poetry workshops circulated a mimeographed document in which they criticized the "almost mechanical" way the experience of the first workshops in Cardenal's community of Solentiname was applied to the entire country. The document was the result of discussions held in another official cultural organization, the Union of Nicaraguan Writers, which is part of the Sandinista Association of Cultural Workers.*

The authors of the document praise the richness and variety of Nicaraguan literature in general and, specifically, Ernesto Car-

denal's "innovative experiment" on the island of Solentiname during the time of Somoza. They take issue, however, with the teaching methods of the coordinator of the workshops (Mayra Jiménez), who relied almost exclusively on the literary precepts of exteriorism (see introduction to Ernesto Cardenal). They also disagree with Mayra Jiménez's assessment of the workshops as "developing a new concept of the poet in the Revolution." They point out that "in principle, political, social and historical poetry is nothing new in Latin American literature. It has been considered an extremely dangerous kind of poetry because one needs a high mastery of expression in order to preserve quality. And it is *dangerous since it falls so easily into realism or into the language of political pamphlets. . . . The enemies of the Nicaraguan Revolution are neither exteriorism nor surrealism—to cite two opposite literary techniques. We believe that it is healthy for diverse literary currents, within the framework of the revolution, to be cultivated simultaneously with an open mind."*

The document ends with the assertion that the authors are "in agreement with the existence of the workshops and support them." The authors' objective, however, is to "reorient" the workshops' methodology with the ultimate goal of strengthening the Revolution.

It is in this context, then, that this discussion from Ventana *is so important. It is a way of discussing both the positive and negative aspects of an ongoing cultural process.*

Excerpts from "Between Freedom and Fear"

Rosario Murillo: We're concerned about the development of those poetry workshops. We've discussed it on other occasions. We think it might start to limit creation in Nicaragua, if it isn't doing so already.

Guillermo Rothschuh Villanueva: In Nicaragua there has already been the influence of Cardenal with exteriorism. This influence has grown even more gigantic after the creation of these popular poetry workshops, which try to convert this form into the only form of creation. And what's more, they're trying to create a school. But, on the other hand, within the eruption of the Revolution it's the form that lends itself most readily to express things that certain sectors are trying to say for the first time. In some ways, exteriorism is the most effective form, but we . . . are concerned, because we believe that the results of all this are going to be or already are negative.

Eduardo Galeano: . . . Once creation becomes the right of everyone and ceases to be the privilege of just a few, a revolution can get to know itself much better and can become much more familiar with the reality in which it is operating. Because it is this cultural production that is going to reflect all the contradictions . . . hidden in the belly of reality that couldn't be seen before, since there was no one to see or to talk about them. I think it's important that creation not have dams around it that will block it—especially when you consider that knowledge of reality enables one to change or transform reality more effectively. . . . But that's where the problem begins, because you've got to have some criteria of selection when you start to distribute these new products. It's inevitable. . . . Who decides what's good and what's bad? This is a problem that hasn't been resolved in any of the revolutionary experiences. People have tried a thousand times, a thousand different ways, but the problem remains unresolved, because the problem is deeply political and has to do with the expropriation of the right of creation. In capitalist societies, it's the right of just a few. Only a few people consume and produce art. . . . The road to socialism produces many grave problems that aren't easy to resolve. I have the impression that the *distribution* of cultural products is one criterion not so essential to a revolution. And I'm sure some people are mistaken when they say that it is. If, for example, you go to a socialist country and ask someone: "What has been done in the area of culture?", they'll say, "Before, 13 books a year were published. Now, we publish 13,000." That's very important, but I would say that it's not the most important thing. Because what's most important isn't the distribution of cultural products, but the distribution of the *means* of cultural production, which is something quite different. In fact, it is the heart of the problem if products are going to be distributed. Because otherwise we follow the same relation of creation and consumption that existed previously. By decreasing illiteracy and increasing social equality the Revolution has only multiplied the numbers involved in that relation, giving a greater quantity of people access to cultural products. But there continue to be some people producing for others. I think the key lies in distributing the means of cultural production with as much freedom and flexibility as possible—without being scared of the results. Because if the results produce conflicts, we should welcome these conflicts as part of reality. It's not that there are people with bad intentions who want to invent conflicts in order to disrupt the Revolution's process. On the contrary, I believe that it is a healthy sign in a revolution to take into account the conflicts that, in reality, exist and not to lay the blame on the person who witnesses the conflict. An ugly face isn't the mirror's fault! It's true. Just like those ugly girls used to say, "The mirrors nowadays are terrible!" And here, of course, reality has a thousand conflicts and a thousand contradictions—but they are precisely what enriches reality. To conceive of reality as something with a single dimension and motionless would be very mistaken.

In general, in previous revolutionary experiences, I have the impression that things haven't functioned at the level of the revolution's vitality—I said this publicly in Cuba during a meeting with Cuban writers. Because we have to be honest, we shouldn't lie. Because if one goes around playing things up and saying "How marvelous, how marvelous!", one isn't doing the revolution any favors. I think we have to defend the revolution in the face of its enemies, but within the revolution we have to demand the most rigorous honesty. Certain things must be said.

We have the impression that in literature, for example, the cultural reality of the Cuban revolution is less rich than reality itself. In other words, that the vitality, the richness that one finds on the street, in the countryside, speaking with anyone anywhere, has been reflected very little in literature. That's the truth. And in journalism, too, which is another form of literature. In other words, journalism and literature are less interesting, smaller than the reality that, theoretically, they should express. And these are things that should make us think profoundly. Why is the segment that should be the happiest and most ecstatic be, in fact, the grayest? Why? Why are film and graphic arts in Cuba, for example, much more vital than literature? I believe that in a process like the one in which you are living now—this act of giving birth in which you are the protagonists—these things must be taken into account.

Francisco de Asís Fernández: There are also other genres that have emerged with the triumph of the Revolution—such as the testimonial genre. . . . Leaders of the Revolution such as Omar Cabezas and Jacinto Suarez have become writers and storytellers. There are many people who have talked about their human experience during the Revolution. The testimonial genre didn't exist in Nicaragua until now. It has to do with an attempt to evaluate what happened in this country. It is also related to the Sandinista mystique and an historical memory that must be preserved and given its proper place. It's our way of saying: "This is what happened to us, and we don't want to go through it again." . . . We should also take into account that we must not value only what has emerged recently, but make room for what was written before—

the people who produced art before. We can't just forget about what was created before the Revolution. In Nicaragua, generally speaking, what was created before is absent. There's only one current, one definite voice—Cardenal's. But in that same generation, there are three different, firm voices: Ernesto Cardenal, Ernesto Mejía Sánchez, and Carlos Martínez Rivas. And we must re-examine that part of our literary heritage that really isn't present at this time. These three different voices also provide options. If we just stick with Cardenal, that's only one option. What's lacking is a proliferation of options—and that's something that is necessary. Perhaps this is one way to deal with the problem of the workshops: providing them with different options, other voices. In this way, new creative perspectives will emerge.

Juan Gelman: I think it would also be important to teach the professional craft of being a poet in the workshops: how to write sonnets, *romances*, etc. And after that let them write in free verse or write sonnets. Let each person find his own voice. That's really important. Not everyone should have to be an exteriorist poet. There might be a marvelous surrealist.

Francisco de Asís Fernández: What Juan says is very important. . . . We need all the breadth possible—a wide horizon.

Rosario Murillo: I think we have to assume some responsibility in all this. We haven't been able to confront the problem. To a certain extent we've been inhibited and haven't faced up to the problem except on an individual level. It could very well produce a shock among some of the people in the Ministry of Culture. But I think that if we're so concerned about this matter, we should bring it up honestly and seriously with the appropriate people. . . . We should set up a discussion and work from a constructive perspective.

Eduardo Galeano: There isn't a single language of the Revolution because there isn't a single language of reality. Reality has a thousand languages—and so does Nicaragua. . . . The Revolution is a revelation because it uncovers a hidden reality. . . . Based on the historical experiences we're familiar with, there is something here that concerns me a great deal: the fear that isn't a fear of the Revolution or the fear one finds at the highest levels of leadership in revolutionary processes; it's the fear and panic of the *lower* government officials—*not* the panic of the leaders. Why? Because, generally the lower government official in a revolutionary process tends to be conservative. He tends to become frightened by the conflicts that call his beliefs into question. Such a person is generally a very petty bourgeois—who doesn't reflect a revolution itself. . . . That's a problem all revolutions must face: the paralyzing bureaucrats! . . . That's why I think it's very important for the Revolution to rescue the multiplicity of life with all its conflicts.

Francisco de Asís Fernández: We've said before that the Revolution hasn't set down themes or forms for the production of art. Never. On the contrary . . . *everything* goes, within the Revolution. That's an enormous freedom. Here there must be, and there is, the freedom to write love poems or poems about whatever the poet wants to say. But there does exist something called self-censorship. Many people think that they have to write poems about the Revolution. And this idea has been promoted in the workshops. The writers think the Revolution and its leaders must be praised. This kind of thing diminishes the world of art and the world of the Revolution.

Rosario Murillo: About what was said concerning self-censorship, fear, and conflicts, I think we often make the mistake of writing, painting, and singing without presenting problems or difficulties. When we refer to the work set forth by the Revolution, we praise and glorify it. I've seen what has been written about the militia, for example. And everyone says the militia is marvelous, but no one talks about how hard it is to join the militia, that it demands discipline, tenacity, sacrifice. No one talks about how hard it is to pick cotton. . . . I think we have to overcome that kind of presentation of paradises, because we should tell about the difficulties, the vacillation, the fears, and how hard it is to conquer them. . . . When you do an interview, you find that people tend to forget the difficulties they had to face in order to fulfill certain responsibilities. And they appear like superheroes. This takes away from the testimony's strength since it lacks any basis in reality. There's a certain amount of fear, nostalgia, and suffering. And conquering all this is what makes great things and great men and women. In the Revolution this too is valid.

Mayra Jiménez

At the suggestion of Ernesto Cardenal, Costa Rican-born Mayra Jiménez arrived in 1976 at the community of Solentiname located on an island in Nicaragua's Great Lake and founded the first popular poetry workshop. She was forced to leave Nicaragua in 1977 for the same reasons as Cardenal, after repression by Somoza's soldiers made it impossible to remain there. The workshops, whose members were mainly Sandinista combatants, continued in Costa Rica during the last phase of the Nicaraguan insurrection. Since 1979, Mayra Jiménez and the Ministry of Culture have organized many popular poetry workshops in Nicaragua—and not without a certain amount of controversy. Due, in part, to criticism of her teaching method, Mayra Jiménez returned to Costa Rica in 1983. The poetry workshops have been reorganized in the Ministry of Culture and now function under the auspices of the Ministry's twenty-four Popular Cultural Centers throughout Nicaragua. I interviewed Mayra Jiménez in her office at the Ministry of Culture in July 1982.

I'd like to know how you organized the first workshops.

The idea of creating a poetry workshop in Solentiname began to emerge slowly after conversations between Ernesto Cardenal and me. Ernesto had told me in Caracas that in Solentiname there was a movement of "primitive" painting and that the Gospel was studied. Then I asked him why, since he was a poet, there wasn't a group of poets from the community of Solentiname. In those sectors there had always been excellent poets. And Ernesto told me that he hadn't tried to work with poetry because he didn't know how to go about it. He told me that he knew how to work with the Gospel and with "primitive" painting, but not with poetry. Then he asked why I didn't try to form a group of poets there—of campesinos, above all. He knew I had previous experience in that I had held poetry sessions with children and adolescents in Costa Rica. We succeeded in forming a large group of child poets who wrote excellent poetry in San José in a conservatory dedicated to the arts. So, with that experience, I went to Solentiname at the end of 1976. During the first Mass of that first Sunday in November, Ernesto told all the people that anyone interested in poetry should stay afterward so that they could talk with me. He told them that I had come from Caracas and that I wanted to talk with them about poetry. We were hoping that three or four campesinos from the community would stay. But we were surprised when almost thirty stayed. Then I had a conversation with them and explained what I wanted to do. I asked them if they were familiar with Ernesto Cardenal's poetry and they told me that they had never even heard it. Ernesto had been living in the community for more than ten years and he had never read them his own poetry or anyone else's. I was really surprised that they weren't familiar with Ernesto's poetry and began by reading it to them. We began to read and comment on it. They liked it a lot, and we began to study other poets like José Coronel Urtecho. They had met him but didn't know that he wrote poetry either.

Wasn't José Coronel living just across the border, in Los Chiles?

Yes. Every so often he came to visit. And these campesinos from Solentiname got to know the best Nicaraguan poetry and the poetry from other parts of the world. I remember that once we had a session where Ernesto translated Chinese poetry directly from English. They liked the Chinese poetry a great deal. That was an afternoon when I had asked Ernesto to join me and the campesinos, because Ernesto did not meet with us very often. Just our group met. He stayed in his ranch, writing, and I met with the campesinos below in the church near the lake. But that afternoon I invited him to come down, and that was when he translated the Chinese poetry. Very quickly they began to write poems without my telling them to write. I just guided them and we all made comments, and they read, too. It was a spontaneous thing. Here's a nostalgic poem about life there called "In Solentiname" by Iván Guevara:

Everything was far away in Solentiname: the lake,
the islands, the church where we all used to meet
on Sundays, the avocado trees
next to the plaza where we played soccer,
the afternoon with the lake calm or barely
rippling from a shark's fin,
or a bird taking a bath, the moonlit nights
when we played or danced with Nubia's
sisters, and I played my guitar and sang
some songs by Silvio Rodríguez
or Carlos Mejía.
We won't see Ernesto leave his house
anymore and go down to the dock with his knapsack,
the hat, some book in his hand and the robe he used
to celebrate Mass in Papaturro.

The first poems were discussed between the author and myself. Later, other poets, other compañeros, began to participate in the discussion until the poetry became a collective and social phenomenon where the campesino poets themselves discussed different lines, rejected them, changed them, transformed them. The result was the book that you're familiar with called *Poesía campesina de Solentiname* (Campesino Poetry of Solentiname). It contains all the work from those months. That was the first experience.

How long did those poetry workshops last?

Until the beginning of 1977. A few months later, the preparations for the insurrection that was to come intensified. In October, the barracks of San Carlos were assaulted. Then, for obvious reasons, Ernesto Cardenal himself asked me to leave Solentiname and go to Costa Rica since I could no longer remain in Nicaraguan territory. This poem by Olivia Silva, the mother of six Sandinista guerrillas, is about the repression that year:

October 12, 1977

It's four o'clock. We have to leave to cross the lake.
Waves, wind, more waves.
Solentiname, with its freshness, was to the north—
herons flying to the high grass
the rice being harvested
the fields smelling of corn
the screaming birds.
And all that, I think, raped by the National Guard

the way they raped Amanda Pineda.

We continued the workshop in Costa Rica after the assault on San Carlos. A number of poets who belonged to the group had participated in the attack. As a result, three were taken prisoner: Elvis Chavarría, Felipe Peña, and Donald Guevara. And the others went to Costa Rica, because sometimes they got sick or needed training. So, clandestinely in Costa Rica, we continued the workshops in 1977, '78, and '79 until the triumph of the Revolution. Of course, all the poets were no longer there. Sometimes there were only one, two, or three people. I met with whoever could make it. I met with Felipe Peña during the first months. Then he was murdered by the Guard, just as Donald Guevara and Elvis

Chavarría were later murdered. The workshop had several geographical locations: in Nicaragua and later Costa Rica, and, later, again in Nicaragua.

Now that you're in free Nicaragua, have your methods for organizing the workshops changed?

No. The method is still the same. It consists in gathering all the people of a community for a first meeting where the work that will be done is explained: literary training and literary technique through apprenticeship to improve poetic quality.

Are these meetings conducted primarily in Managua or in other cities as well?

In other provinces of Nicaragua also—of course we always work in the most proletarian sectors. We work in the villages and other places that are most representative of the people. That's where we ask the people to attend a first meeting. After the first meeting, the people who attend find out who's interested in attending further sessions. Sometimes twenty attend, sometimes fifteen, sometimes fewer. It doesn't matter how many remain. The important thing is that in a certain village or city we discover who the poets are. Sometimes they are poets who haven't written a single line. But they feel like poets, they like poetry, and they want to write. They didn't dare before. When they come to the first meeting, we tell them that poetry isn't an art that belongs to a small minority, to an elite, but that art is the people's. The people have to produce that art. Then they immediately begin the process of poetry, in abundance, because they always wanted to but hadn't. They thought being a poet was a condition just for a few.

About how many poets are participating in the workshops now?

535 poets have passed through the poetry workshops. That's how many we've discovered in the different sectors of the national territory. Fifty-three poetry workshops have been opened all over Nicaragua: in the north (Palacagüina, Condega, Estelí), in the south (Río San Juan), in the east (Bluefields), and in the west (Diriamba, Masaya, Granada). All over Nicaragua, poetry workshops have been created. I figure that the anthology that I'm preparing right now contains no less than 200 poets—which is quite representative of the poetry workshops. There are poets who enter the workshops, acquire a certain technical knowledge about writ-

ing poetry, and then, after a while, leave; but the people in the book are the more permanent poets.

Have the workshops produced a conflict with other cultural workers in Nicaragua?

There have been differences in conceptions about art in Nicaragua between the people in the workshops and some sectors of the other poets. There wasn't really a conflict, just different ideas about what art should be. This is very understandable, because in a revolution not everyone has to have the same concept of what art is. There can be different ways of focusing on art, none of which contradict the Revolution itself. And I think the argument that occurred between the poets of the workshops and some poets who were writing before the establishment of the workshops was a natural argument. At no time were any attempts made to undermine the Revolution.

What kind of poetry is being written in the workshops?

Well, we've always said that the poetry workshops produce work that is eminently revolutionary. Within that concept it has certain characteristics. The poets, owing to their proletarian origins, use a concrete, simple, and direct language. The images are closely related to the immediate reality and the experience of each of the poets. And that gives the poetry a certain tone. It's a testimonial poetry, a historical poetry, a geographical poetry. A permanent feature of this poetry is the presence of nature: the names of trees, rivers, and birds. The poets also use the names of our leaders, the heroes who died, the people who served in the literacy and health brigades. The names of the brothers and sisters who didn't survive are used, too. In other words, this poetry has gathered in verse a large part of Nicaraguan history before and during the war and now, after the triumph.

Does this kind of poetry have anything to do with "exteriorist" poetry?

Yes, undoubtedly there is a closeness between the poetry of the workshops and the poetry that in Nicaragua is called "exteriorist." The fathers of this kind of poetry—Ernesto Cardenal, José Coronel Urtecho, Fernando Gordillo, and Leonel Rugama—have, in a way, become the fathers of these poets in the workshops. What I mean is that the characteristics of these great poets from before the victory have a great deal in common with the characteristics of the younger poets who appeared after the triumph. There are certain differences. The poetry isn't identical, but, yes, they share certain qualities just as the new poetry has a lot in common with other kinds of poetry. Certain poets in the United States, for instance, use a language that is fairly concrete, descriptive, and conversational. I'm referring to great poets such as William Carlos Williams and Carl Sandburg. If that's exteriorism, the poets in the workshops are undoubtedly exteriorists in this sense.

Metaphors and elaborate concepts must be scarce in this kind of poetry.

They are not very prevalent. It isn't a conceptual or metaphorical poetry. But we don't have anything against the metaphorical or the conceptual. It's simply a phenomenon. The poets in the workshops all have proletarian origins. They're campesinos and workers. The language they use for poetry is the language they use in their everyday lives. They write that way and nobody tells them they have to. When they begin to discover that they have things to say, the language they look for to express these things comes from their day-to-day life. What we do in the workshops is give the language the profundity it needs to become art. In the development of the poem, line by line, the language is given a depth and poetic dimension. If it didn't have these qualities, it would be prose. And poetry can't be confused with the strict form of prose. Even though the poetry is conversational and anecdotal, it's still poetry. It has all the strength and dimension of verse. It's not prose. We intensify these things in the workshops with criticism, self-criticism, commentaries, and technical work.

It seems to me that many times the language of the people is naturally metaphorical—especially in the legends and stories the grandparents tell the children. Does this kind of language enter the poetry of the workshops?

No, for very understandable historical reasons. We shouldn't forget that it hasn't been very long since the triumph. The poets who are in the workshops are young people between the ages of seventeen and twenty-six and are poets who have participated in the war. They're all combatants. The experience that forms the major emotional burden at this time is still closely related to what was going on before, during and after the war. A good example is the poem "July 19" by Manuel Adolfo Mongalo, who belongs to the Diriamba Poetry Workshop:

The sky was clear.
It was cold.
We were all Sandinistas embracing each other
because of the news of our triumph
over the National Guard a few hours before.
It was July 19, 1979.
We came in a caravan of trucks—
hundreds and hundreds of young, happy combatants.
When we entered the city of Granada at two in the morning,
the people got out of bed.
They gave us coffee, tamales, beans, and cheese.
Girls were running back and forth.
Mothers were looking for some face on each of us.
Others were crying (some compañeros did not return).
That night was pure emotion: joy, triumph, Revolution!
I walked to the Hotel Alhambra.
Sadness—smoking rubble, burnt land, and houses.
A dog in the middle of the street cried and cried.
It was close to death.
I walked. My eyes filled with tears.
And just before it died, that animal licked my hand
as if it were trying to tell me it couldn't die.
That's what happened with Victor, my compañero,

when we were in the same trench in Ostayo.

They haven't looked for ways to bring to their poetry that other world related to legend and myth, superstitions, symbols, and the interpretation of different phenomena. That's the way these young people write and there's no reason to force them to change. It wouldn't be natural for them to look for that other world. They're searching for a testimonial form they can use to express in poetry their most recent experiences.

My last question, Mayra, is: what importance do the workshops have for the cultural development of Nicaragua?

I think that the workshops have formed a landmark in the history of Nicaraguan literature, because, for the first time, the people themselves produce their own art. The most important Nicaraguan poets, from Darío until now, have produced an art for the people with a revolutionary awareness. They wrote so that poetry could be enjoyed by the people. This is the case of Ernesto Cardenal and others. Now, on the other hand, the people themselves produce their art, the workers themselves say the things they feel and live. I think that with the appearance of the poets in the workshops, with the discovery of the poets in the different cities and villages, we have been able to convert from theory into practice what any revolution would sustain: art is from the people, should come from the people, be enjoyed by the people, and be produced by the people. Now, art isn't *for* the people but *from* the people. This, in my opinion, in terms of cultural development, is very important for a revolution. This is especially true if one takes into account the fact that the majority of the poets in this revolutionary process have been combatants. What's more, all the poets who have been working with us in the workshops are incorporated in the Revolution through different activities. I'd like to add that 50% of the poets who are in the workshops also belong to the Armed Forces: the Popular Sandinista Army, the Air Force, the police, or State Security. In other words, they have very important jobs in the Revolution and, at the same time, produce their poetry, saving through poetry all their daily experiences in the revolutionary process. I think this is a unique phenomenon in the world.

Alvaro Urtecho

Alvaro Urtecho, to a large extent, fits into the Romantic tradition of Wordsworth, Hölderlin, Rilke, and Stevens. The subjective qualities of his work create a kind of private religion divorced from the demands of public life. When the Romantic poet touches on social themes there is often an inherent opposition to materialism and the abuse of those who labor in a material universe (e.g., Blake's "London"). But everyday life in Nicaragua, filled with material shortages as well as threats of violence and invasion, is an extremely politicized series of crises that can only be resolved collectively; so, under these circumstances, it is difficult for a writer to maintain a conception of the artist as aristocrat or pariah.

Alvaro Urtecho was born in the city of Rivas in 1951. After the Sandinista victory, he returned to Nicaragua from Costa Rica where he had been doing graduate work. He taught at the National University in Managua and later at the Regional University in Estelí, where I interviewed him in July 1982. Since then, owing in part to the high level of politicization among the faculty, Alvaro Urtecho has returned to Rivas to write. Many of his poems and essays have been published in the cultural supplement, Ventana.

What relation does your childhood have with the formation of your poetry?

I believe that every poet is in some way a receptacle for maternal space—that maternal space the great German poets, Novalis and Rilke, have transmitted to us. A maternal space forms a poet in such a way that it conditions his work. I don't mean that a poet isn't going to cultivate himself or renew himself through books or events, but I believe childhood is fundamental.

For you, that maternal space was Rivas, the city of mangoes and cocoa, in the southern part of Nicaragua, wasn't it?

Yes, that's where I lived with my family: the lake near Rivas, the sea. This is very important for the sense of infinity in my poems. Rivas is located in a valley. This valley is, at the same time, surrounded by water. Five kilometers from Rivas is the Great Lake of Nicaragua, and fifteen kilometers from Rivas is the Pacific Ocean. That sensation of distance and infinity always invaded me. The sensation of space has always been present in my poems—especially in my early work. There is a geographical conditioning from the experience of my childhood in the city of Rivas: that sensation of something unlimited, something beyond us and at the same time beyond history.

Can you tell me something about your family background? Were there other writers in your family?

Of the writers dedicated to literature, there's José Coronel Urtecho, a relative of mine, a great former of generations and of teachers. Nevertheless, I should say a little about the fact that there is an intellectual tradition in my family apart from the figure of Coronel. Granted that these people weren't professional writers, there were people in my family who dedicated themselves to writing, who had a certain period of splendor in the era of the Conservatives at the end of the last century, and who, little by little, declined because they couldn't adapt to the life of materialistic and pragmatic capitalism that came to Nicaragua. José Coronel Urtecho compared me to those members of the Urtecho family from Rivas and told me that the Urtechos are like the Buendía family in *One Hundred Years of Solitude*: a family that lives in a past of memories. I remember the house of one of these relatives: those chairs with the legs of a lion, the great medallions. Everything breathed nobility and antiquity.

When did you first leave the maternal space of Rivas?

It was in Managua, before the earthquake, where I first experienced the symptoms of alienation in modern society. It was also in Managua that I wrote my first serious poems. In Rivas I wrote many things, but they were all very dependent on the Romantic poetry of Victor Hugo, Espronceda, and, of course, Darío. In Managua, my poetic world seemed to take shape. Then I went to Spain to study philosophy and literature between 1970 and 1975. When I was in Madrid, I met Carlos Martínez Rivas.

What was he like at that time?

Always dynamic. Always a great conversationalist. Once he took me to see Vicente Aleixandre. We went in, and Carlos grabbed Aleixandre's hands like this, kissed them, and said: "Onorate l'altissimo poeta," as if he were Homer greeting Virgil in Dante's Inferno. Aleixandre, who is good friends with Nicaraguan poets such as José Coronel and Pablo Antonio Cuadra, said: "Carlos, please. Why are you doing this?" "And why not?" said Carlos, a perfect courtier. "No, Vicente. Here in Spain one kisses the archbishop's hands, so why not kiss the hand of a great poet?" And Aleixandre loved that, even though Carlos was making fun of him. Carlos Martínez is not famous in Spain. Only the people deeply involved in poetry know him. But the great poets are scared of him because they know that Carlos knows more than they do. With the contacts Carlos had in Spain, he could be more famous right now than Octavio Paz, even though, in my opinion, he isn't as precocious. Paz, in his memoirs, describes Carlos Martínez as "a small rodent with brilliant eyes."

It's clear that philosophy forms an integral part of your work. Which philosophers have had the most influence on your poetry?

I'd like to say something before continuing with that theme. Using the expression "philosophical poetry" is repugnant to me. I think poetry is poetry *without* any adjectives. The term "philosophical poetry" makes it seem as if philosophical treatises were being put into verse. Nothing could be further from what I do. I write the kind of poetry that can be read by anyone who reads poetry. It's absolutely existential, based on life. There's my poem "Lazarus," for example:

The dry uproar of a sudden lifting of doves
shook my steps.

As if something

had escaped from my flesh,
its root surprised.

As if they lifted the slab from the corpse
I guard and through the world
it journeyed now with nothing in its hands.

To write this kind of poetry, it hasn't been necessary for me to read and to study philosophical treatises.

But you have read them?

Yes, I've read the great philosophers and feel very close to the representatives of phenomenology and existentialism—that subterranean and free current of thought that comes to us from Seneca, passes through Pascal, and is prolonged in Nietzsche, someone I really admire for his radical independence, independence of thought and judgment. He is a man who did not submit to schematic thought. Nietszche is a man of the future. He is the kind of intellectual who will be produced when humanity is more liberated from its constraints. He's a philosopher, but he's also a poet—a mixture. Consider the case of Hölderlin and Schiller in German Romanticism: their works are based on Kant's thought. But one can't say that Hölderlin depends on Kant's thought in the same way that, to a certain extent, Schiller does. Hölderlin's intuition is dialectical, like Hegel's intuition. When I hear "philosophical poetry" it bothers me. I'm concerned with philosophy, not because I think that philosophy has the truth. There's as much truth in poetry as in philosophy. There's as much truth in religion as in mythology or in eroticism or in love. Nor do I believe in the systematic zeal of philosophy. Nothing could be farther from the way I am. I haven't received a degree in philosophy, because I'm incapable of undertaking an academic thesis. Philosophy is an extension of my own poetic spirit. The concerns in my poetry lead me to make incursions before the police-like faces of the professional philosophers. Ever since I was a child, I've had this encyclopedic desire to know everything.

What exactly is it that you dislike about being identified as a philosopher?

I'm from a small country where people have this mania for giving things labels. For example; "exteriorist" poetry. Just because it occurred to Coronel and Cardenal to give that name to a tendency of poetry that is descriptive and epic. So, now we have exteriorists (the epic poets) and interiorists (the lyric poets). The whole thing is really foolish since neither exteriorism nor interiorism exist in chemically pure states. Great poetry is a mixture of the two tendencies. Take Carlos Martínez, for example. He is an interiorist but an exteriorist as well. It is precisely in him that I see the most select example of the poet in Nicaragua. In other words, Carlos Martínez is someone who embodies a whole poetic tradition.

In what sense?

In the sense that he has what is epic and what is lyric—in "Two Murals: U.S.A.," for example. He is someone who describes the world, but not like a photographer, nor as a chronicler as Cardenal does, not like a journalist, and not like a sociologist. He does it like a poet. In other words, he presents landscapes, he presents paintings, expressing his subjectivity.

What kind of poetry do you identify with?

My preference is fundamentally lyrical and moral poetry. Meditative poetry. The great Spanish baroque poets have served me a great deal: San Juan de la Cruz, Fray Luis de León, and Quevedo. But of these, I think I'd stick with Quevedo, because he expresses himself in such a concentrated way. Quevedo succeeds in expressing in a few lines what philosophers have been trying to say in their enormous treatises. The poetry that has struck me the most, apart from the incomparable seventeenth century, is the great Romantic poetry in English and German. It's less rhetorical than ours. Our Hispanic tradition is filled with little, useless words. The Germans and the English, on the other hand, get to the heart of the matter. They think more. It's not by accident that England and Germany have produced philosophical thought. I remember that Octavio Paz once said that in Latin America literary criticism doesn't exist because philosophy doesn't exist.

Why doesn't philosophy exist? Because of the language itself?

Well, yes. There are two tendencies involved here. Some believe that, yes, there is philosophy if we understand philosophy as I understand it: non-systematic philosophy. But if we understand philosophy as great systems of coherent thought, then of course not. But we have Ortega y Gassett and Unamuno, who are people who have thought. And in our Latin America we have Octavio Paz, someone who besides being a poet is also a philosopher.

Where do the erotic elements in your poetry come from?

For me, eroticism is absolutely inseparable from death. Eroticism is death's sitting room. If, in my poetry, desolation, sadness, and nostalgia predominate, eroticism is the other face. Just as life is the other face of death. I address these themes in "Grotto":

Moist lips grow silent when
at the bottom of a room the naked
lovers smile, caress, contemplate
enlarge the shadow where love
and death no longer have anything to fear.

But what models do you have? Rilke?

For eroticism, no. Rilke isn't an erotic poet. But Rilke has influenced me a great deal. He is the poet I adore most. Rilke is the culmination of all German Romantic thought that is not only poetry but also philosophy. What interests me about Rilke is the capacity of abstraction in his contemplation. But my eroticism lies in the baroque sensuality of Latin America—in Neruda. He is probably one of the poets I've read most. And of course the great Spanish poetry of the Generation of 1927: Luis Cernuda and Vicente Aleixandre. There is a certain joy in my work, a certain exaltation of life that perhaps could be related to Jorge Guillén, although I don't share his optimism.

Where do you locate yourself in Nicaraguan poetry?

Perhaps in regard to economy and verbal precision, I'm close to Carlos Martínez. But in regard to thought and my conception of the world, I feel much closer to Ernesto Mejía Sánchez, a nostalgic, profoundly pessimistic, and dissolute poet. And, of course, Joaquín Pasos. And now that we're on this, since I'm a metaphysical poet, we'd have to take into account our great Alfonso Cortés. I share his mystical, celestial attitudes. I also know that Pablo Antonio Cuadra has moved me deeply: he is one of the Nicaraguan poets who impresses me most for his great inspiration, inspiration from Nicaragua. Pablo Antonio is a tragic man. Not in the sense that he is a nihilist (which, to a certain extent, I am) but tragic in the sense that he gives us an emotive vision of the human being. The campesino in Pablo Antonio Cuadra's work, stripped of its folkloric and localist aspects, is a campesino filled with tragedy. He is as tragic as the Greek tragedies.

In your poetry I see a great internal coherence, a sustained meditation on great ontological or eternal problems. Does this attitude still pervade your work?

Yes. One could say that I'm a poet of a single chord in the sense that in my poetry, as in the poetry of Mejía Sánchez, there is a great coherence. There is an organic intellectual structure. I am a poet of personal anguish. I write directed by my obsessions. That's why it doesn't occur to me to write an epic or sociopolitical poem. Nevertheless, I have great desires to be more human in my poetry. I want my poetry to reflect the social reality more. I want it to. But I haven't found the poetic form in which to do it. Since I'm so wrapped up in the musical structure of the lyrical poem, it's difficult for me to use and introduce all those colloquial words. I'd like to get out of this, perhaps with a novel or a book of short stories. At this time, I'm at a stage of revision.

Did you finish the previous stage with your poem "Cantata"?

The "Cantata" left me reduced to ashes. After the "Cantata" I stopped writing. I haven't written poetry for three years. I wrote the "Cantata" in the summer of 1979 in San José, Costa Rica during the time when the preparations were being made to overthrow the dictator in Nicaragua. It's a poem in which I put all my strength, all my youth.

There seem to be signs that your poetry will go through a transformation. I'm thinking about your poem "Elegy before the Remains of the Hero," which you wrote shortly after the triumph of the Revolution.

You can't imagine the anguish I felt when I wrote that poem. I was on the verge of abandoning it. I had just arrived in Nicaragua fifteen days after the triumph. I found out that the next day, a Sunday, the remains of a young guerrilla named Ricardo Talavera Salinas, who had been assassinated by the Guardia, were being brought to Rivas. A delegation from the Popular Sandinista Army was also coming. Since Ricardo had been a friend of mine, I asked his family for permission to read an elegy. For me—someone so wrapped up in subjective, abstract, existential poetry—the idea of writing, in so short a time, a poem related to Nicaraguan reality was a torture. I felt guilty and didn't think I was going to finish it. But all the memories of my childhood—the lake, the mangoes, the cows—helped me give the text a poetic dimension that otherwise would have been impossible. High-ranking Sandinista officers arrived at the cemetery. All the people from Rivas were there, too. Before the coffin was lowered, someone said: "Silence, please. The poet from Rivas, Alvaro Urtecho, is going to read a poem." I read my elegy. You know that at burials people don't usually clap. But when I finished the poem, there was incredible applause. Then the Popular Army with the salvos! Afterward, Pablo Antonio Cuadra published the poem on the editorial page of the newspaper, together with a poem by Ernesto Cardenal. That was during the time when *La Prensa* was Sandinista. Perhaps that poem I wrote is the beginning of a new kind of humanistic, committed poetry for me.

Since you're such a pessimist, does your poetry fit into the context of the Revolution?

The only thing I can tell you is that if a revolution is genuine, it must absorb what is genuine. If a revolution is great and authentic, it has to absorb all existing forms of artistic expression. A revolution that limits artistic expression, that sets down rules, can't be a genuine revolution. It might be an economic revolution, perhaps.

What should be the role of a writer in a revolutionary society?

I think that however revolutionary a society may be, however dedicated to goals of justice and liberty, a revolutionary government is never going to change the critical attitudes of artists. I believe that the artist is a person who has a critical awareness that is irreducible to any system. That's why I think that the best way for a writer to participate in a revolutionary society is by using permanent criticism. The permanent revolution. And not to become a bureaucrat, please! The worst thing for a culture is when a writer becomes a bureaucrat, a policeman, an inquisitor at the service of the Sacred Writings—even if the sacred writings are Marxist-Leninist. Freedom of expression is a conquest by the people, a conquest that humanity has tried to achieve throughout the centuries. Even if this government is revolutionary, any government that eliminates freedom of expression, justifying its actions for whatever beautiful, philanthropic ends, is mistaken. That repression will clash sooner or later with the independent position of the writer.

Rosario Murillo

One of the most prominent voices in new Nicaraguan poetry is that of Rosario Murillo, born in 1951. Her literary work is inseparable from her cultural activism. In 1974, along with the well-known Nicaraguan folksinger Carlos Mejía, she helped establish the urban group of "committed" artists called Gradas. She is currently the Secretary General of the Asociación Sandinista de Trabajadores de la Cultura (ASTC; Sandinista Association of Cultural Workers) and the editor of the cultural supplement Ventana. *She is married to Nicaragua's recently elected president, Daniel Ortega, and is the mother of eight children.*

Her recent book of poems Amar es combatir *(To Love Is to Fight) gathers the best work from two volumes published before the Revolution. Her book* Un deber de cantar *(A Duty to Sing), published in 1981, won the 1980 Leonel Rugama poetry prize. The urgency of her poetry reflects the artist's duty to sing until, as Muriel Rukeyser said in* The Life of Poetry, *"the peace makes its people, its forests, and its living cities; in that burning central life, and wherever we live, there is the place for poetry. And then we will create another peace."*

I interviewed Rosario Murillo in her office at the Casa Fernando Gordillo in January 1984.

Will you describe the structure and some of the activities of the Sandinista Association of Cultural Workers?

We make up what we call the trade union organization of Nicaraguan artists. We're organized in different unions, all of which are grouped together in the association. It's a union of unions: writers, painters, musicians, dancers, people who work in the theater, photographers, and circus workers. Each union has its group of directors and secretary general. The secretary general of each union comprises the coordinating committee of the association. And the secretary general of one of the unions is elected to be the secretary general of the entire association. We support ourselves with membership fees and on the basis of international relations. But, of course, our budget is limited. Above all, our work consists in helping creators disseminate their work, both here and abroad. We also enable the artist to take part in the new and active life of the Revolution by gradually removing the dictatorship's obstacles to the artist's social function. We actively try to solve the artists' material problems with living and working conditions, health, recreational needs, etc. Because of our success in these areas over the last two years, one of our most important goals for the near future is "professionalization." What I mean is that the best artists in their respective fields would receive a salary to develop their work professionally.

Right now there's an exhibition here at the Casa Fernando Gordillo entitled "Painting Rubén Darío's Poems." Where did this idea come from?

That idea came from the artists themselves. Before the triumph of the Revolution, some of these same artists had a similar experience in making paintings based on poems and other literary texts. After the Revolution, Rubén Darío was declared a national cultural hero who would be celebrated annually. As their contribution to this celebration, the artists chose a fragment of a poem or prose piece with which they identified, and then they painted their impressions. We hope to extend the application of this idea to other Nicaraguan poets.

I'm wondering if a North American public understands the phenomenon of the circuses in Nicaragua. Could you say a little about these small, independent groups that travel all over the country?

In Nicaragua, there are almost thirty private circuses, all of which are miserably poor. For the last year and a half, we've been working on creating a union of circus artists and workers. Generally speaking, the circus owners and workers belong to just one family. Despite our budget limitations, we would like to help them buy their materials—things made locally and whatever can be imported. This is necessary so that the circuses can develop technically. Until recently, the circus, was probably the most neglected art form. It wasn't considered part of our culture or even considered art under the dictatorship. Through workshops and seminars, we've helped change that attitude. After all, the circus is a fundamental part of the people's recreational habits and plays an important role in the creation of a child's magic universe. We regard the circus as the art form with the greatest potential for reaching the people. That's why we've devoted so much time to this cultural phenomenon and have created La Carpa Nacional (The National Big Top) where artists and their invited guests from both here and abroad perform. We do the best we can in spite of limited costumes, equipment, lighting, sound, etc. The circus requires a daily heroism. Not just because of limited funds and personnel, but because of the dangerous conditions under which circus people work. For example, throughout Nicaragua and even at La Carpa Nacional, they work without a net. It's terrible the way the artist risks his or her life every day. One fall could mean death. We're doing everything we can to buy a net. But in the meantime, we're very satisfied with the level of professionalism these artists have achieved—especially when we see how well they're received by the people. The circus provides a refreshing vital element that helps relieve the tension in this time of war.

Where, exactly, does the money come from to finance the ASTC's activities? From the government?

No. As I said before, we finance ourselves with our resources based on membership fees and international sources. To give you an example, the materials we import for the plastic arts are purchased with the 20% donated by each artist when he or she sells a painting. The same money helps us put out publicity and catalogues. Materials are sold to the artists at cost. Not all artists are in the same category. There are amateurs or beginners, associated with the organizations of the masses and Centros Populares de Cultura (Popular Cultural Centers). The Ministry of Culture gives these people the necessary technical and organizational skills. The artists who belong to the ASTC have more experience and are more well known in a professional capacity. We still haven't perfected the mechanism by which these compañeros are selected. And we are less demanding about the qualifications of potential members in areas that are relatively new to Nicaraguan culture, such as dance and theater. Artists aspire to join, since belonging to the association signifies a certain level of recognition. Our goal of professionalization, which includes providing the artists with a living wage, is another advantage for members.

What kinds of activities do you have planned for the fiftieth anniversary of Sandino's death and for the rest of the year?

Whew! All kinds of activities! We have a very intense work plan. A music festival for electronic music, campesino music, the New Song, the Testimonial Song. We'll be having contests in painting, drawing, photography, choreography. The Second National Dance Festival. An exhibit of all the different kinds of costumes used in Nicaraguan folk dancing. A theater festival with productions, workshops, and meetings of people from all over Central

America. Meetings for directors of museums and art galleries from all over the continent. The artists will paint murals—one each month in different barrios and villages. An international circus festival. You can see that we'll be busy. There will also be a forum on "Art and Literature Five Years after the Revolution" this July. It's going to be a discussion to evaluate the cultural work that's been done since the triumph.

Who will participate?

We're in the process of figuring out how this activity will be organized so as to include all the organizations in the cultural field—the different ministries, the ASTC, the representatives of the organizations of the masses, people from the government, etc. We want to clarify what we've achieved, discuss our problems and limitations. We want more people to understand the importance of cultural activities in the Revolution. For the leaders of the Revolution this importance is very clear. It's also well defined for a great majority of the people. But sometimes there's a lack of understanding concerning the specificity of cultural work on the part of the intermediate sectors. A classic example of this is some barrio coordinator who doesn't understand why it's necessary to create optimum working conditions, say, for lighting and sound. This person might think it just isn't important. Sometimes here at the ASTC we find ourselves overwhelmed with requests like: "We need a mural here, right away"; or, "Tonight we need a presentation on such and such a topic." And we don't have time to incorporate these things in our plans because the requests come on such short notice. That's why there has to be a greater understanding about the specificity of cultural work since it requires concentration and discipline. Another objective of this forum is to make specific proposals concerning the Revolution's cultural politics. It's something that the National Directorate has been asking of us for the last four years.

I recently saw a very interesting article in a Swedish magazine called Cuestión. *It's about the cultural brigades sent by the ASTC to the war zone on the border with Honduras. Part of the article was entitled "With Rubén Darío beneath the Bullets." (See Appendix)*

There's a tradition here of the artist and intellectual participating in the struggle of the people. While it's true that the artist can train in the militia or get involved in productive work such as the harvest of coffee or cotton, the artist's main contribution to the defense of the Revolution lies in the field of culture itself. This is something we deeply value. We see it as a continuation of the participation of the artists in the struggle waged by Sandino and the Frente Sandinista. That's why, when the emergency arose, we asked ourselves: "What should be our role?" First of all, we have to be ready militarily—just like the rest of the people—to defend this Revolution, with weapons in our hands. But we also have to defend the Revolution as artists. And so we go to the different fronts of the war as artists, to do theater, music, poetry, and painting for and with the soldiers. And if we have to go into combat, then we do it. There have been several brigades of this type and they will begin again in March. The last three months have been spent planning cultural activities for February and the rest of the year. What's most important about all this is that we've emerged even stronger in our conviction that art plays an important role in the Revolution. I don't know if there's any other country in the world where the plans of war consider the artist as an artist—not just as a soldier. Those of us at the ASTC have our own plan in the case of direct military intervention on the part of the United States. All artists will be enlisted. Our battalions are formed. We know we'll be going with our guitars, brushes, and books, and, at any given moment when it's necessary to fight, we'll be shooting as well. We're going to give of ourselves, and nourish ourselves so we can continue creating. An artist isn't revolutionary just because he paints a member of the militia with a rifle on his shoulder. The best Nicaraguan artists are abstract painters. Cultural workers in Nicaragua are involved in the Revolution in their neighborhoods or in cultural brigades and remain in direct contact with the everyday experiences of life as a part of the masses. It doesn't matter what style or form they choose to express themselves. Their work is revolutionary because it comes from a human being who's living the Revolution in all its manifestations. Each artist has his or her particular way of expressing "defense" or "production" or "love" or "death" or "suffering" or "joy," and we respect that. Absolutely. We believe that the direction an artist's work takes in the Revolution is something that opens the doors to creativity and to the imagination and to the development of multiple forms and styles. We don't want to run the risk of monotony and uniformity in art. On the contrary. All the doors to individual creativity based on the collective experience are open.

You're also a poet and have published several books. How has your poetry changed according to your historical experience?

One's individual work has to be the product of one's personal experience within the collective experience. I'd call the language I used initially in my poetry clear, simple, and elemental. It had a lot to do with my personal development. Those were my first attempts at poetry. But it also had to do with my links to the revolutionary movement at that time. My literary exercises formed an open part of my revolutionary militancy. Along with Carlos Mejía, David Macfield, and others, I helped establish the group called Gradas, which was the first experience in Nicaragua of cultural work for the masses. My poetry was imbued with the necessity I lived every day of communicating with the masses. In Gradas we tried to change the concept of cultural work so that the people were not merely receivers but *creators* of culture. At that time, my poetry responded to the need of immediate communication. When the situation changed and we were persecuted and jailed by the dictatorship, we adopted a different strategy. My work went from being open to playing a part in the clandestine network. Publicly I had to be careful so that the place where I lived could be used as a safe house. On the one hand, my poetry reflected the need to continue communicating; but, on the other, I had to communicate in such a way as not to catch the attention of the censors who read the newspapers. I had to keep myself "clean" in terms of security in order to protect the compañeros in my house. My poetry became wrapped in images. In some cases I was fortunate, in others not. I'd throw out many of the poems from my book *Sube a nacer conmigo* (Arise and Be Born with Me). One of my strongest early poems is "Christmas Carol," which I dedicated to my son, killed in the earthquake on December 23, 1972.

I walk today
with the pain of childbirth in each step
with my womb torn apart
and the pieces of motherhood
flying through empty spaces
I walk, moaning
squeezing the iron bars
clenching my teeth
biting my tongue
I go dressed in mud
I go covered with stones and time
I have a face of rubble and hair of fire

I carry the pain of childbirth in each step

I feel my son sprouting from blood
I feel my skin hanging
my veins are tied in a single knot
there's a child spilled in the night.

What's curious is that when I had to leave Nicaragua, something inside of me hurt—like I was going to die. I didn't know how long the struggle in Nicaragua was going to last and how much time would pass before I would be able to come back. I gathered everything I had written and I published it. Everything. Without any criteria of selection. It was a kind of testament. Now I'm sorry about having published much of that material, because it's imperfect. While I was working in the Frente, I had complete freedom to write whatever I wanted. At no time did the Frente orient one's literary work by saying: "Write a poem about this and don't publish a poem about that." Never. It's a personal decision. When I left Nicaragua, I didn't write anything during 1977. In 1978 I began to take up writing a little, and in 1979 a bit more. This is the material I published in *Un deber de cantar*. Later, in 1980, I began to write much, much more. I'm working on a book now, but the problem is that I don't have time to polish the manuscript. When one has reached a certain level of development in esthetic expression, one becomes demanding of oneself. And I'm holding the book back because I know it's not perfect and I could work on it more if I only had the time. The danger of the vortex we're living in, of the deaths, massacres, impacts of one form or another, is that events are much more rapid than one's capacity to assimilate them. And this incapacity sometimes leads one to scorn the importance of certain poetic principles since there's no time to assimilate anything, much less the time one needs to write. I'm creating poetry because the Revolution is great poetry. I know this and agree with this, but I also feel the responsibility of giving the people my written work—and good work. It's a risk one takes. Amidst the infinite tasks one takes on, one has to struggle in order to find the equilibrium for writing, reading—even if it means staying up all night. That's what I've decided to do, because I work here until 8 or 9, or sometimes later. But I read every night even if I have to go to sleep at two in the morning. That means it's hard for me to get up the next day and be at work on time, but I don't feel guilty, because I know that the work I do at night is also part of the Revolution. It would be unrealistic to think about doing a lot of writing in times like these. Perhaps in another five years, when everything is more organized and there are other compañeros who can assume these tasks that we're doing now, we'll be able to say: "Okay, now I'm going to write." I think the poetry I'm working on now is more serious, perhaps. It reflects my own maturity. Before, I was more volcanic, explosive. I thought more about what I had to say than how to say it. Now I not only think about how to say it but also about how everyday personal things are not necessarily poetic material. I think maturity helps one distinguish whether or not what's elemental and ordinary is beautiful and good material for a poem and when it's just something unimportant that won't communicate anything to anybody. I'm learning these criteria.

How can cultural relations between the United States and Nicaragua be improved?

There are infinite possibilities. We've been working on some of them for the last year and a half. We've established some excellent links with the film industry in Hollywood. We have some very good friends there.

Did you meet with Jane Fonda and Ed Asner?

Yes, with them, and with Burt Schneider, Warren Beatty, and others. They are important because they have the potential for reaching such a large portion of the North American people. But we're also very interested in the exchange of experiences between writers, dancers, actors, and musicians. These people can, of course, clarify the Nicaraguan Revolution for the people of the United States. But we're just as interested in knowing what North American artists and intellectuals are involved in as creators. And we want them to know what we're doing here in Nicaragua. This communication is a vital necessity.

Appendix

With Rubén Darío beneath the Bullets

By Fernando Butazzoni, correspondent for Cono Sur Press

(Translated from an article that appeared in Spanish in the Swedish magazine Cuestión, *June 1983).*

One day, the Germán Pomares Cultural Brigade organized by the Sandinista Association of Cultural Workers arrived in Teotecacinte, near the border with Honduras. They were to perform cultural activities on the different fronts of the war. Among the members of the brigade were musicians, clowns, jugglers, folk dancers, and a playwright who was in charge of reading poems at each of the presentations.

After talking with the military chiefs of the zones of operations, the people of the brigade marched to the place called El Limón to give their first performance. It was truly a moving experience to see the soldiers' faces when they saw the equipment, guitars, and colorful costumes used by the girls during the performance being unloaded from the truck. The men were tired, worn out, after long, sleepless nights on guard duty. Their feet hurt from boots that were too new or too old but always wet. They calmly sat down under the palm trees to enjoy the show. Rolando Steiner, around fifty years old, who has written several fine plays, was in charge of beginning the presentation by reading poetry of Rubén Darío, Cabrales, and other Nicaraguan poets. A few minutes before, he had confessed to me that he was a little nervous because of the insistent and increasingly close machine-gun fire.

When it was announced that the show was about to begin, there were several mortar explosions about 300 meters from where we were sitting. Then Rolando took two steps forward and began to read a poem by Darío while at the same time the gunfire grew more intense behind us. He also read a poem by Coronel Urtecho, and, finally, enthused by the proximity of the fighting, another poem by Darío. . . . When he had finished, there was a long silence, broken by an endless burst of machine-gun fire. None of us moved. We were calm, almost entranced by Darío's poetry. At last, someone reacted and began to clap. Then the rest of us clapped. Rolando Steiner came and sat down beside me, sweating and happy. He leaned over and whispered to me: "Let's see, *compa*, lend me your rifle for a while."

Selected List of Useful Publications

Anthologies

Nicaragua lírica. Ed. Augusto Oviedo Reyes. Santiago, Chile: Editorial Nascimento, 1937.

Poesía nicaragüense. Ed. María Teresa Sánchez. Managua: Editorial Nuevos Horizontes, 1948 (Premio Rubén Darío); rpt. 1965.

Nueva poesía nicaragüense. Ed. Orlando Cuadra Downing. Madrid: Seminario de Problemas Hispanoamericanos, 1949.

Poesía revolucionaria nicaragüense. Mexico City: Ediciones Patria y Libertad, 1956; rpt. 1968.

Cien poesías nicaragüenses. Ed. Rolando Steiner. Managua: Ediciones El Pez y la Serpiente, 1963.

"Poesía nicaragüense contemporánea." Ed. Margaret Randall and Sergio Mondragón. *El Corno Emplumado* 15 (1965): 35-72.

Poesía nicaragüense post-dariana. Ed. Ernesto Gutiérrez. León: Cuadernos Universitarios 3, 1967.

Nueva antología de la poesía nicaragüense. Managua: Ediciones El Pez y la Serpiente, 1972.

Poesía nicaragüense. Ed. Ernesto Cardenal. Havana: Casa de las Américas, 1973; rpt. Buenos Aires: Ediciones Carlos Lohlé, 1973; and San José, Costa Rica: Ediciones El Pez y la Serpiente, 1976.

Poesía escogida de mujeres nicaragüenses. Ed. Fanor Téllez. León: Cuadernos Universitarios 15, 1975.

Nicaragua in Revolution: the Poets Speak, A Bilingual Collage. Ed. Bridget Aldaraca, Edward Baker, Ileana Rodríguez and Marc Zimmerman. Minneapolis, MN: Marxist Educational Press, 1980.

Poesía campesina de Solentiname. Ed. Mayra Jiménez. Managua: Ministerio de Cultura, 1980.

Poesía atlántica. Ed. Julio Valle-Castillo. Managua: Ministerio de Cultura, 1980.

Poesía de las fuerzas armadas. Managua: Ministerio de Cultura, 1981.

Poets of Nicaragua, A Bilingual Anthology: 1918-1979. Ed. Steven F. White. Greensboro, NC: Unicorn Press, 1982.

"Poemas miskitos contemporáneos." Ed. Carlos Alemán Ocampo. *Nicaráuac* 8 (Oct. 1982): 165-179.

Talleres de poesía: antología. Ed. Mayra Jiménez. Managua: Ministerio de Cultura, 1983.

Antología general de la poesía nicaragüense. Ed. Jorge Eduardo Arellano. Managua: Ediciones Distribuidora Cultural, 1984.

A Nation of Poets: Poems from the Sandinista Workshops of Nicaragua. Ed. Kent Johnson. San Rafael, CA: West End Press, 1985.

Magazines

Nicaraguan Perspectives (Berkeley, CA)

Nicaráuac (Managua)

El Nuevo Amanecer (Managua—supplement to *El Nuevo Diario*)

El Pez y la Serpiente (Managua)

Poesía Libre (Managua)

La Prensa Literaria (Managua—supplement to *La Prensa*)

Ventana (Managua—supplement to *Barricada*)

Studies

Arellano, Jorge Eduardo. *El movimiento de vanguardia de Nicaragua, 1927-1932*. Managua: Imprenta Novedades, 1969; rpt. Managua: Ediciones de Librería Cultural Nicaragüense, 1971.

Arellano. *Panorama de la literatura nicaragüense*. Managua: Ediciones Nacionales, 1977, 3rd rev. ed.; rpt. Managua: Editorial Nueva Nicaragua, 1983.

Cardenal, Ernesto. "Ansias y lengua de la nueva poesía nicaragüense," *Nueva poesía nicaragüense*. Ed. Orlando Cuadra Downing. Madrid: Seminario de Problemas Hispanoamericanos, 1949: 7-99.

Cardenal. "Lo qué fue Solentiname. Carta al pueblo de Nicaragua." *Casa de las Américas* 108 (1978): 158-160.

Cardenal. *La revolución y la paz mundial*. Managua: Ministerio de Cultura, 1980.

Cardenal. "The Revolution is a Work of Love." *Nicaraguan Perspectives* 3 (1981): 4-7, 22-24.

Cardenal. *La democratización de la cultura*. Managua: Ministerio de Cultura, 1982.

Coronel Urtecho, José. *Prosa*. San José, Costa Rica: EDUCA, 1972.

Coronel Urtecho. *Tres conferencias a la empresa privada*. Managua, 1974.

Coronel Urtecho. "Resistencia de la memoria." *Revista del pensamiento centroamericano* 150: 98-107.

Cuadra, Pablo Antonio. "Los poetas en la torre (memorias del movimiento de vanguardia)." *Torres de Dios*. Managua: Ediciones de la Academia Nicaragüense de la Lengua, 1958: 143-208.

Dorfman, Ariel. "Tiempo de amor, tiempo de lucha: la unidad en los *Epigramas* de Ernesto Cardenal." *Texto Crítico* V, 13 (1979): 3-44.

Eitel, Jim. "Revolutionary Artists, Revolutionary Morale." *Nicaraguan Perspectives* 7 (Winter 1983): 18-21, 41.

Farías, Victor. "La poesía de Ernesto Cardenal." *Araucaria* 15 (1981): 101-118.

García Marruz, Fina. "Una nueva poesía popular en Nicaragua." *Nicaráuac* 11 (May 1985): 195-221.

Ministerio de Cultura. *Hacia una política cultural*. Managua: Ministerio de Cultura, 1983. (Speeches by Bayardo Arce, Tomás Borge, Carlos Núñez, Luis Carrión, Daniel Ortega, Sergio Ramírez, and Ernesto Cardenal.)

Randall, Margaret. *Cristianos en la revolución*. Managua: Editorial Nueva Nicaragua, 1983. Translated as *Christians in the Revolution*. Vancouver, B.C.: New Star Books, 1984.

Randall. *Risking a Somersault in the Air*. San Francisco, CA: Solidarity Publications, 1984.

Ryan, Tony. "On Cultural Resistance: An Interview with Greg Landau." *Nicaraguan Perspectives* 7 (Winter 1983): 25-28.

de la Selva, Salomón. *Sandino: Free Country or Death*. Ed. Jorge Eduardo Arellano. Managua: Biblioteca Nacional de Nicaragua, 1984.

Smith, Janet Lynne, "An Annotated Bibliography of and about Ernesto Cardenal." Tempe, AZ: Center for Latin American Studies, Arizona State University, 1979.

Tirado, Manuel. *Conversando con José Coronel Urtecho*. Managua: Editorial Nueva Nicaragua, 1983.

Valdés, Jorge H. "The Evolution of Cardenal's Prophetic Poetry." *Latin American Literary Review* 23 (Fall-Winter, 1983): 25-40.

White, Steven. "Toward Cultural Dialogue with Nicaragua." *Third Rail* 5 (1982): 45-64.

Woodward, Kenneth L. "Conversation with Father Ernesto Cardenal." *Geo* (March 1984): 14-24.